The Mail-Order Food Book

The Mail-Order Food Book

by
William I. Kaufman
Produced by
Jean-Claude Suarès

Designed
by
Elizabeth
Thayer

Grosset & Dunlap
A Filmways Company
Publishers ● New York

Contents

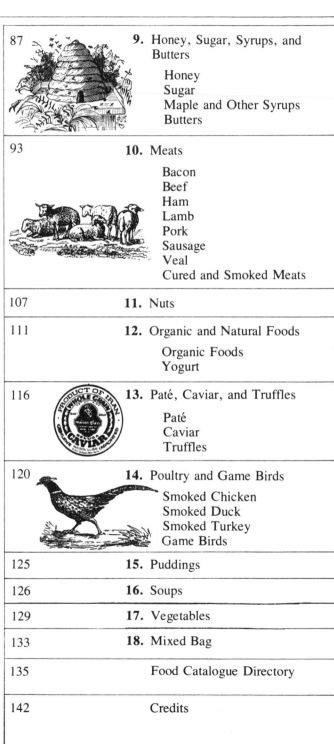

Guidelines for Ordering by Mail

All the mail-order firms mentioned in this catalogue are reputable and will stand behind their merchandise. Nevertheless, neither I nor my publisher is responsible for any transactions between the purchaser of this catalogue and the firms included. In order to make your mail ordering a bit easier, I suggest that you adhere to a few simple rules. In twenty-five years of buying mail-order merchandise, I have never had a negative experience as long as I have followed these rules.

1. If at all possible, write for a catalogue from the firm whose foods you are interested in purchasing.
2. We live in a world of constantly changing prices. If I have indicated the price of a food as $1.00, and when you order it you find it is $1.25 or $1.50, chalk it up to inflation. On the oher hand, prices on certain items may go down when the mail-order firm is paying less for its raw materials.
3. Allow time. If you are willing to pay the price, firms are happy to send merchandise via air mail. Surface mail costs less and takes longer. When ordering from overseas, allow a great deal of time if you want to save money and use surface mail.
4. Be certain to request shipping rates and sales tax and remember that there is a duty to be paid on most items from overseas.
5. Unless you know the taste of a food product, order only a minimum amount.
6. Keep in mind that NO ONE is trying to take advantage of you. Mail-order firms are just as interested in satisfied customers as your local store. Deal with them in the same manner.

Inclusion in this catalogue does not constitute an endorsement by the author or the publisher.

The Mail-Order FOOD Book

Foreword

I'm a catalogue nut. I love catalogues. I collect them, gather and assemble them, browse and dream with them. I also use them. Catalogues satisfy my needs for everything from knitted caps to Vermont Cheddar.

This catalogue is designed for your browsing and dreaming—and using. It should satisfy all your needs in the food area, including some you didn't realize you had. It is a veritable super supermarket at your fingertips, offering you access to over 2,000 food items from around the world. It provides a fast and easy reference for the gourmet, and a trigger for the imagination of the gourmet-in-training.

People who live in big cities can easily get fresh pasta, wild rice, acacia honey, strudel dough, Deglet Noors, and organically grown cereals. But for those who live in other areas, these foods, and such delicacies as smoked turkey, marzipan, and sambul, have been no more than dreams. No longer. Now they are no farther away than a phone call or a postage stamp.

For party-giving the catalogue is superb. Exotic fruits and nuts, candies and pastries, soups and hams are all here inviting you to become the hostess-with-the-mostest. It allows you to turn a Saturday night dinner party into a celebration of note. For example, by sending the date and exact time of your party to the Seafood House, you can sit back and relax. The live lobsters will arrive right on schedule—just minutes ahead of your guests.

The catalogue is indispensable for gift giving. Not only does it make gifting pleasant and easy, but it also assures that your gift will be remembered long after others are forgotten. You will rate high on the guest list when you remember your host or hostess with a tin of Pate de Foie Gras with Truffles from Maison Glass in New York or a Coalport Jar filled with English Breakfast Tea from Fortnum & Mason in London.

Are there some hard-to-please people on your gift list? How about impressing your husband's boss with a special box of delectable chocolates from Fauchon in Paris? After all, they are only $40 a pound! What family will not sing your praises while drowning their Sunday pancakes in Pure Vermont Maple Syrup? What cheese lover will not be delighted with a wheel of Colby from Wisconsin? Not to mention those delicious citrus fruits from Florida and the apples and pears from the orchards of Oregon? The selection boggles the mind. It runs the gamut from a pint of Maine Apple Jelly to a $500 jar of Royal Iranian Caviar.

Want to be good to yourself? This catalogue makes it easy. If you have always wanted to sample smoked turkey but didn't know where to find it, now you do. Try it. It may be the first time, but I'll wager it won't be the last. Simple oats, cornmeal, and other grains and wheats from the shelf of your local market can't hold a candle to the fresh-from-the-mill variety. Try tempting the members of your family with real ScotchStyle Oatmeal from one of the suppliers. Once they relish ''real'' oatmeal you'll have a hard time keeping your pantry stocked. Ever dream of experimenting with a sourdough starter? Well, now you can, and with an honest-to-goodness piece of the original Sourdough Jack's, from Alaska.

Live and eat gloriously—via this Catalogue!

William I. Kaufman

1.

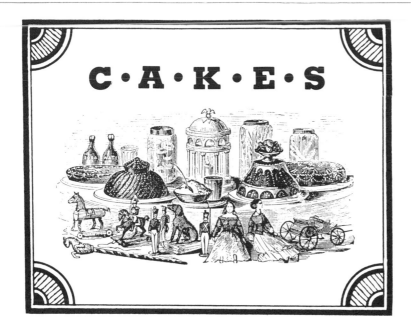

Banana Rum Ring

Made with butter and lots of fresh bananas, light rum, whole eggs, almonds, and rum. Packed in a reusable golden tin.

1½ lb. $6.50

Pepperidge Farm

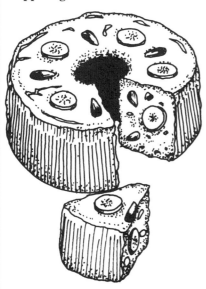

Cheesecake

Plenty of smooth cream cheese, farm-fresh whole eggs, and churned creamery butter mixed in small batches and baked in the Bear Creek Bakery results in this sheer perfection of taste and texture. A delectable two-pounder gives 12 generous servings. Beautifully hand-packed in a gold-embossed gift box—and guaranteed to arrive fresh and perfect!

Order Gift No. 338 $9.95 delivered

Harry and David

Chocolate Almond Rum Ring

A combination of chocolate and almonds mixed with a swirl of rum to create an exciting flavor.

1½ lb. $6.50

Pepperidge Farm

The Original Chocolate Dobosh Torte

Available nowhere else. Swiss Colony originated the Dobosh Torte many years ago, using only the finest rich chocolate for their special Dobosh Cream. They still make this torte the authentic Old World way, from traditional recipes and with pride in their standards.

Ship. wt. 2 lb. (1¼-lb. torte) $4.50
Ship. wt. 3 lb. (2-lb. torte) $6.50
Ship. wt. 4 lb. (3¼-lb. torte) $9.95

The Swiss Colony

Christmas Cakes

Rich, moist plum cakes that are baked early in the year, matured with French Brandy, and suitably decorated with Almond and Royal icing before dispatch.

2-lb. cake $12.90
3½-lb. cake $16.40

Egertons

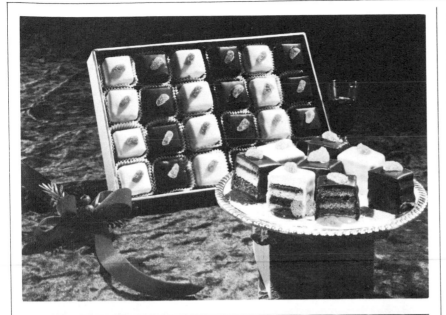

Colomba

An Italian dove-shaped cake that is popular for Easter, Colomba was first made to commemorate the Lombard victory over Frederick Barbarossa in the battle of Legnano, Easter 1176. Available in Motta and Alemagna brands. Only available in April, May, June.

1 lb. 2 oz.
1 lb. 10 oz.
2 lb. 3 oz.
3 lb. 4 oz.
4 lb. 4 oz.

Manganaro Foods

Prices obtainable on request from supplier.

Cordial Cakes

Colorful confections with alternating layers of butter-rich cake and delicious liqueur-flavored fillings—raspberry, rum, crème de cacao, apricot, orange and brandy—all covered with light and dark chocolate. Selection contains 24 Cordial Cakes.

Net wt. 14 oz. $3.95

The Swiss Colony

Cream Cheese Cake

A blending of country-fresh eggs, creamy cheese, and the most delicate flavorings baked in a golden flaky crust. To complement the flavor, two jars of Cherry Topping are included. Available November 15 until Christmas.

2½ lb. $8.95

The Swiss Colony

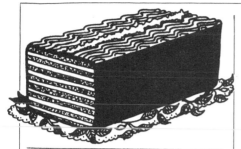

Creme de Menthe Torte

A fabulous torte with a refreshing mint flavor. There are seven thin layers of fluffy chocolate cake and six layers of butter cream touched with Crème de Menthe. Gift boxed.

Net wt. 1¼ lb. $4.50

The Swiss Colony

Dessert Cakes

Imported from Europe, these delicious dessert cakes come in two boxes, four cakes in each box. Made with sugar, flour, eggs, milk chocolate, and Grand Marnier liqueur.

8½ oz. $5.50

Pepperidge Farm

Dobosh Medley

A delightful blending of the richest cake layers with light cream fillings. There is Chocolate Dobosh Cream for Fudge Nut and Dobosh Tortes, Rum-flavored Butter Cream, and Mint Butter Cream. Beautifully packaged in varicolored foil and ribbons. Included are Crème de Menthe, Rum, Fudge Nut, and Chocolate Dobosh Torte.

Net wt. 2 lb. 14 oz.

The Swiss Colony

> Prices obtainable on request from supplier.

Dundee Cake

F & M Dundee Cake in a tin. A rich cake made from selected dried fruits, Bigarreaux cherries, pure butter, and eggs. Topped with roasted almonds.

2-lb. cake $24.00. Post and packing $4.00

Fortnum & Mason

Gingerbread House

A real gingerbread house, with its roof all covered with sugary snow! It's made of gingerbread and has stick-candy trim for real windows and a door. It's big, too; stands 8 inches high on 11 x 8-inch base.

Regular house $8.50
Extra large house (twice as much!) $11.95

The Swiss Colony

Mr. Guinness's Cake

Ingredients include the famous Guinness stout, the best Sultana raisins, fruit peel, walnuts, and mixed spices. One enthusiast described it as "like eating dreams."

Net wt. 2 lb. $10.60

Egertons

Pandoro

A specialty cake from Verona, Italy, the city of Romeo and Juliet. Available in Motta or Alemagna brand; the price is the same for either one.

1 lb. $4.25
2 lb. $7.50

Manganaro Foods

Panettone

The traditional Italian cake for holidays and festive gatherings. A high, fluffy semisweet cake that is light, dry, and lemon-flavored. Stuffed with raisins and citron. This cake stores well and comes packed in a colorful box. Specify Motta or Alemagna brand; the price is the same for either one.

1 lb. $4.25
2 lb. $7.25
4 lb. $12.50

Manganaro Foods

Panforte Di Siena

A round flatcake thick with candied citron, orange, sugar, and almonds blended with pure fine flour. Cinnamon and vanilla are added to make its characteristic aroma.

1 lb. $4.40
7 oz. $3.00

Manganaro Foods

Paradise

A "slice of Hawaiian Paradise." A blend of macadamia nuts baked with juicy chunks of Island Pineapple make a Macadamia Nut Pineapple Loaf.

1¼ lb. $5.95

Figi's

Pistachio Torte

The most luscious confection your taste buds ever went wild over, delicate Pistachio Torte is a combination of white cake layers and the creamiest pistachio-flavored butter cream. A coating of fine chocolate and pistachio nuts.

Net wt. 14 oz. $4.25

The Swiss Colony

Royal Kona Coffee and Hawaiian Happy Cake

A wonderful combination: original Hawaiian Happy Cake from Kemoo Farm served with incomparable Kona coffee. Bring back beautiful memories of the islands.

1 lb. coffee and 2-lb. cake $13.50 postpaid in U.S.

Kemoo Farm Foods

Sacher Gateau

A rich chocolate cake filled and topped with chocolate icing. . . .

1 lb. cake $4.00. Post and packing $2.00.

Fortnum & Mason

Stollen

A German coffee cake shaped in a long loaf and baked with unbleached flour. Loaded with citrus fruits and raisins washed in butter.

Net wt. 1½ lb. $6.50

Great Valley Mills

And More Stollen

Another German coffee cake, this one served on a hand-painted wheat pattern ceramic bread platter.

2 lb. $14.95

Great Valley Mills

Yule Log

The most elegant Christmas dessert to grace any holiday table. This fluffy chocolate cake is filled with a smooth butter cream ever so delicately flavored with Crème de Cacao liqueur.

Nt. wt. 1½ lb. $6.45

The Swiss Colony

FRUITCAKES

Bourbon Cake

Here's a Bourbon-laden loaf cake filled with walnuts, whole eggs, creamery butter, raisins, and nutmeg.

1 lb. 4 oz. $7.95

Pepperidge Farm

Christmas Breakfast Cake

A big, beautiful cake, filled with choicest ingredients, this one is ready for Christmas appetites. Each carefully handmade cake has an unusual taste achieved by blending fruits and rich butter-batter with a unique almond swirl.

Net wt. 1½ lb. $5.95

The Swiss Colony

Christmas Fruitcake

This prize-winning formula is the result of many bakings, and comes with a ''best you've ever tasted'' guarantee. It's a rich blending of honey, butter, pecans, golden pineapple, sweet cherries, and fine English walnuts. Arrives in a gift tin.

Net wt. 2 lb. $6.95

The Swiss Colony

The Mail-Order Food Book

Creole Fruitcake

An old-fashioned Louisiana delicacy, this cake is baked with a symphonic blend of nuts and glazed fruits—and with that special New Orleans touch. A unique feature is its individually wrapped slices. It's a great cake for family fare; even better for gift giving. The two-pound and four-pound cakes come in decorative tins.

1 lb. $4.95
2 lb. $10.75
4 lb. $17.00

Kate Latter's

DeLuxe Fruitcake

This cake's appeal is explained in two words: Great Flavor. Prime-harvest cherries and fruits from the Pacific Northwest, France, Italy, and Hawaii are blended into a rich batter crunchy with native pecans. "DeLuxe" is unique in that it is custom baked just for you; every order receives individual care. It is hand decorated and gently packed. Recognized everywhere, this cake arrives in a "keepsake" gift tin that assures perfect delivery and ideal home storage. A gilt-edged guarantee is enclosed with each cake.

	Price per Cake		
Size	1–24	25–99	100 or more
2 lb.	$6.45	$6.25	$6.05
3 lb.	9.10	8.80	8.50
5 lb.	14.70	14.20	13.70

For surface mail delivery from Texas to foreign countries, allow 6 to 9 weeks. Add $2.00 per cake for foreign postage. For shipment to Canada, allow 3 weeks and add $1.75 per cake.

Collin Street Bakery

Gourmet Fruitcake

A careful blending of the finest imported rich red French cherries, Spanish almonds, Malaysian pineapples, and French Charbert walnuts slowly aged in superior Bourbon, Rum, and Brandy, with just enough cake to hold all these luscious fruits and nuts together, have combined to produce this masterpiece of baking. A taste of honey. A treat the whole family will enjoy and remember. And an ideal way to say "Thank You" to relatives and friends.

Three-pound and five-pound cakes are cellophane wrapped and gift packaged in a reusable metal container. One-pound and two-pound cakes are double wrapped in cellophane and silver foil and packaged in an oblong gift box of red leatherette.

	Price per Cake		
Size	6–49	50–99	100 or more
1 lb.	$4.95	$4.45	$3.95
2 lb.	7.95	6.95	6.45
3 lb.	9.95	8.95	8.25
5 lb.	14.95	13.50	13.35

Above prices F.O.B. Nebraska, Los Angeles, New York.

Individual mailing and postage:

1 lb. $1.25; 2 lb. $1.50;
3 lb. $1.75; 5 lb. $2.00.

Butterfield Farms

Great Valley Fruitcake

This is a genuine homemade fruitcake made with the maximum of fruit, rum, eggs, butter, and brown sugar and only the minimum of flour.

2-lb. $7.50

Great Valley Mills

Hawaiian Pineapple Macadamia Nut Cake

This buttery cake, chock full of juicy Hawaiian pineapple and exotic macadamia nuts, is made from an exclusive and original recipe and comes bakery fresh in a gold-foil gift box. This 1½-pound loaf cake freezes nicely, slices neatly, and serves 15 slices.

Order Gift No. 386 $6.95 delivered

Harry and David

Holiday Fruitcake

This is a rich brandy-laced loaf filled with pineapple and pecans and plump, dark raisins—with orange peel and tangy-tart citron added. No artificial colors, flavors, or preservatives.

1½-lb. loaf $7.50
2 1½-lb. loaves $14. 95

Pepperidge Farm

Irish Fruitcake

This is another cake made by the famous Ormeau Bakery established in Northern Ireland in 1875. The recipe for this rich fruitcake includes the use of Marsala wine. Comes packed in a sealed tin.

Net wt. 1 lb. 12 oz. $11.70

Egertons

Kentucky Bourbon Fruitcake

A traditional fruitcake made the way only Kentuckians make it—loaded with 100 proof Kentucky Bourbon—this one is baked to perfection and beautifully decorated on top with the choicest fruits and nuts. It comes in a flavor-sealed vacuum-packed can.

Net wt. 1 lb. 2 oz. $6.40

Broadbent B&B Food Products

Koinonia Fruitcake

A tradition-tried-and-true cake! The batter with fresh eggs and quality flavoring makes just enough cake to hold the fruit and nuts together. There is no citron or grapefruit peel for a bitter aftertaste. But there is a special blending of cherries, dates, raisins, orange and lemon peel, and pineapple from the finest European and South American sources. And, of course, there are lots of Koinonia pecans. All this is glazed with a delicately flavored apricot coating.

Tin:
2½ lb. $6.95
1 to 4 cases (12 cakes per case)
    $73.20 each

Box:
3-lb. cake $6.35
1 to 4 cases (12 cakes per case)
    $66.00 each
1½-lb. cake $3.45
1 to 4 cases (12 cakes per case)
    $37.80 each

(Minimum order to one address $5.75)

Koinonia Products

Macadamia Monarch

Two pounds of Happy Cake, crunchy with delicious macadamia nuts, coconut, and bite-sized pieces

of glazed pineapple, plus four tins of Royal Hawaiian Macadamia Nuts.

As above $17.50 postpaid in U.S.

Kemoo Farm Foods

Our farm is tucked back in the Dummerston hills just far enough off the beaten path to give one the "feel" of the natural beauty of the Vermont countryside. We hope this small brochure will give you an idea of our farm and products and that you will visit us and see the vegetables, fruits, flowers, cheese, salami, maple syrup, jams, jellies, pickles and an array of other items all produced and sold with great pride. We will attractively package and mail any item or combination that you choose. Our price list is available, if not enclosed in this brochure; and a map (back page) will speed you on your way whenever you wish to come. We look forward to seeing or hearing from you.

Maple Fruitcake

Add this to your fruitcake repertory. Made from a special blending of superior and delicious fruits and flavored with Hickin's pure Vermont maple syrup and wine. A taste treat any time of year.

½ lb. $2.50
1 lb. $3.85
2 lb. $7.50
4 oz. cupcake $1.50

Hickin's

Miniature Fruitcakes

Includes 24 individual, decorated fruitcakes made with glacé pineapple, Hennessy Brandy, regular and unbleached raisins, pecans, walnuts, cherries, almonds, and pure creamery butter.

1 lb. 5 oz. $8.95

Pepperidge Farm

Priester's Pecan Fruitcake

This fruitcake is made from a treasured heritage recipe enhanced by Priester's own special formula for aging and mellowing. Luscious dates, sun-ripened raisins, candied

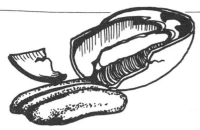

pineapple, and plump glacé cherries are blended with fresh meaty pecans. No mixes, peels, or fillers are used. Cake is molded into a loaf form for paper-thin slicing. A wonderful treat with coffee, tea, as an afterdinner dessert, or to serve to impromptu guests.

2-lb. box $6.50
2-lb. Pettipoint chest $7.60
3-lb. box $8.50
3-lb. Maytime tin $9.75

Priester's Pecans

Sunnyland Pecan Fruitcake

Loads of fancy, mammoth Georgia pecans set the stage for this Sunnyland cake. They are combined with premium-quality glacé cherries, candied pineapple, tender raisins and dates, and a delicious batter. A truly exceptional fruitcake that slices perfectly every time. It is shipped in an attractive reusable tin and stays fresh for months.

2¼-lb. cake $8.75
Case of 4 shipped to one address
    $30.00
Case of 9 shipped to one address
    $63.75

Sunnyland Farms

Pineapple Macadamia Ring

Sweet pineapple and rare macadamia nuts from the 50th state are combined with a rich butter batter, then brushed with rum for very good eating. Comes packed in a reusable golden tin.

1¾ lb. $7.50

Pepperidge Farm

BISCUITS, COOKIES, AND TEA CAKES

Carr's English Biscuits

These are fine assorted biscuits that come packaged in decorative tins.

Assorted (biscuits for cheese)	12-oz. box	$2.75
Gift Tin "Bless This House"	2-lb. tin	8.95
Gift Tin "Flower Basket"	2-lb. tin	8.95
Table Water Biscuits	12-oz. tin	3.25
"Tapestry" (choice assorted)	52-oz. tin	13.95
Wheatmeal	15-oz. tin	3.25

Maison Glass

Champagne Fingers

Delicious biscuits from France.

7-oz. tin $3.95

Maison Glass

Oblong Shortbread Box

These are thin shortbread fingers made by Ormeau Bakery Ltd., established in Northern Ireland in 1875.

Net wt. 1 lb. $10.40

Egertons

Round Tin Shortbread

Here are thick segments of butter shortbread, packed in an attractive tin.

Net wt. 1 lb. 5 oz. $5.70

Egertons

Petit-Beurre

These are the one and only original petit-beurre (pure butter) biscuits baked by Lefevre-Utile, Nantes. The biscuit makers use nothing but pure ingredients from their own Brittany dairy farms.

1-lb. tin $4.50

Maison Glass

Shaws Biscuits

These are delicious biscuit specialties from the Tyne and Wear area of northern England. Assorted luxury biscuits include Yorkshire Parkins, Honey Crunch, Demerara, Geordies, and Hazeltines. No artificial coloring, flavoring, or preservative is used.

2 lb. 2 oz. Fruitbowl Tin $11.80

Egertons

Verkade's Biscuits

These biscuits from Holland come packed in decorative tins.

Cafe Noir	1-lb. 1½-oz. tn	$5.95
Mocca Sticks	12-oz. tn	5.50
Pride of Holland	15¼-oz. tn	7.75
Royal Mixed	15¼-oz. tn	6.75
Speculaas	13-oz. tn	6.50

Maison Glass

"Truro" Biscuits

This is a distinctive pack containing two drums of Cornish Fairings (crisp and crunchy ginger biscuits), two drums of Cherry Choclets (new biscuits containing cherry and chocolate), one drum of Cornish Shorties (a delightful shortcake), and one drum of Country Maide (a biscuit with a lemon-butter flavor).

1 6-drum pack $13.90

Egertons

Alpine Cookie Tin

These are made with a batter using country-fresh butter and eggs following a prized European recipe. After baking, they are beautifully frosted and decorated with confections and nuts, then packed in a beautiful Alpine airtight tin.

1½ lb. $5.95

The Swiss Colony

Butter Crunch Cookies

A rich butter flavor and tiny nuggets of buttercrunch candy give a real homemade taste. Made with unbleached flour and pure creamery butter, these cookies arrive in a golden tin.

13 oz. $5.50

Pepperidge Farm

Cookie Jars

A big assortment of homemade cookies in a beautiful gift tin ready to fill an authentic country-store jar of clear glass. Comes in 11 varieties.

2 lb. $12.95

The Swiss Colony

Cookie Tin Assortment

Almost three pounds of fancy cookies in seven different delicious varieties including chocolate-topped, molasses, sandwiches, and pirouettes. Comes in a golden cookie tin.

2 lb. 13 oz. $7.95

Pepperidge Farm

Country-fresh Cookies

Homemade cookies that are rich in sweet creamery butter, whole eggs,

and sugar. Baked in unusual shapes of shells, hearts, stars, rounds, and twists, they come with coconut spices or chocolate chips.

1¼-lb. assorted $4.95

The Swiss Colony

Danish Cookies

These are the original butter cookies. And they come in an attractive gift tin.

1 lb. $11.30

Egertons

Dessert Cookies

Babas (4 large rum cakes)	12-oz. tin	$2.25
Chocolate Cups a la Mode (for serving ice cream)	Box of 6	2.50
Crepe Suzette (8 crepes)	13-oz. jar	4.50
Macaroons	8-oz. box	2.25
Mocha Sticks	11-oz. tin	5.50
Petit Babas	24 in jar	3.95
Petit Rum Cakes (16 cakes)	14-oz. tin	2.75

Maison Glass

Hermits

A Cape Cod favorite since the days of the Clipper ships, these cookies are rich with spices and raisins. Packaged in a golden tin with grist-mill design on top.

1 lb. $5.95

Pepperidge Farm

Home-style Assortment

Two pounds of cookies attractively packaged in a colorful and reusable tin.

Net wt. 2 lbs. $6.50

Great Valley Mills

Springtime

Two deliciously light cookies come in this assortment. The famous Cigarettes Russe and a cookie so tender it is called a Souffle aux Amandes.

2 12-oz. boxes $6.95

Pepperidge Farm

Tea Time

A cookie assortment that blends infinite variety and European quality. (It's imported from Europe.) Contains 14 varieties of cookies.

2 lb. 3 oz. $6.95

Pepperidge Farm

Wild Rice Tea Cakes

Fifty choice tea cakes made from selected kernels of wild rice make this a delightfully different treat. The cakes are put up in metal tins, sealed airtight.

7 oz. $3.90

Byrd Cookie Co.

PIES, PASTRIES, AND PASTRY FILLINGS

Pecan Pie

This fine 9-inch pecan pie will amply serve eight people. It's made with whole eggs, butter, honey, unbleached flour, corn syrup, and loads of pecans.

1 lb. 14 oz. $6.95

Pepperidge Farm

Baclava

A confection of walnuts, almonds, and honey wrapped in crisp and flaky layers of paper-thin pastry. An aluminum tray holds individual pieces, floating in honey. Serve cold or heat right in tray.

1-lb. tray $6.98
3 trays $19.00
6 trays $35.00

Paprikas Weiss

Cinnamon-Apple Mini-Danish

This is a small all-butter Danish filled with walnuts and pecans, Swiss apple preserves, and pungent cinnamon. Comes in a golden tin.

1 lb. $6.95

Pepperidge Farm

Cinnamon Sticks

These layers of flaky dough are made with creamery buttery, cream cheese, walnuts, and cinnamon. Comes in decorative golden box.

13 oz. $5.95

Pepperidge Farm

French Pastries

Super Petits Fours of light layers of

cake with the most delicate butter and Dobosh creams—in a rainbow of flavors and colors—these are a blending of the finest ingredients and choicest nutmeats with a rich delicious coating of fine-quality chocolate.

Net wt. 1¼ lb. $5.75

The Swiss Colony

Fruit-Nut Rolls

Like minature Danish, these rolls are made with either apricot or raspberry preserves, pure creamery butter, cream cheese, nuts, and flaky dough. Come in golden tins. State choice of flavor of preserve.

1 lb. $6.95

Pepperidge Farm

Fruit Twirls

Rich, buttery pastry swirls around pure fruit preserves. An assortment of raspberry, apricot, and Swiss apple. Contains fruit preserves, creamery butter, cream cheese, and flour. Comes stored in a decorative golden tin.

15 oz. $7.50

Pepperidge Farm

Linzer Tarts

Tarts are made from crisp, sweet double layers of famous Linzer dough that includes sugar, the yolks of country-fresh eggs, and enormous amounts of butter filled with apricot or raspberry preserve. Each tart is approximately 3 inches in diameter. Specify apricot or raspberry filling.

1 doz. $11.98

Paprikas Weiss

Patko

These "horseshoes" bring you good fortune and a fortuneful of flavor. Yeast-dough pastries are baked according to a traditional recipe that calls for country-churned butter and flower-fresh honey. An egg-yolk glaze provides the tempting golden brown color. Individual 4" x 3"

serving size. Filled with walnuts or poppyseeds. Selection can be assorted; please specify.

1 doz. $9.90
3 doz. $28.00
6 doz. $54.00

Paprikas Weiss

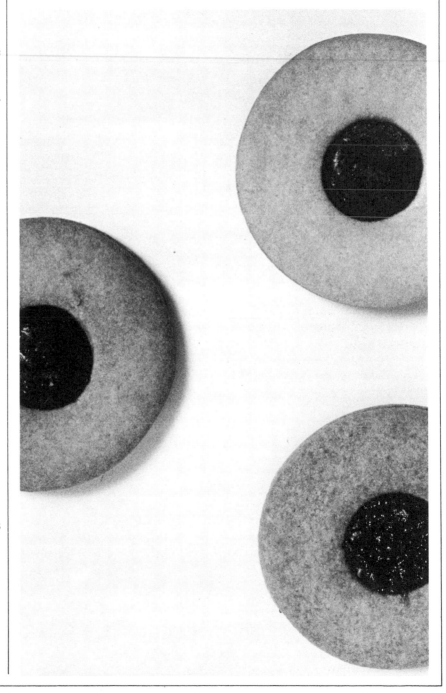

Petit Cakes

This assortment includes 12 each of "old favorites": cordial cakes and petits fours; 6 mini Dobosh tortes; almond, rum, mint, fudge nut, toffee, and chocolate Dobosh. Plus six variflavored French pastries. Light layers of cake with the most delicious butter cream: mint, filbert, orange, strawberry, and two chocolate Dobosh creams.

1¾ lb. $8.45

The Swiss Colony

Petits Fours

These are the most acceptable squares in social circles! Petits Fours look like fancy chocolates, all iced and hand decorated, but inside they're light and fluffy individual layer cakes. No artificial preservatives, but they stay fresh in refrigerator or freezer for up to six months. Great to have on hand for elegant emergencies.

Order Gift No. 374 $7.95 delivered

Harry and David

"Chef Masterpiece" Petits Fours

Liqueur-flavored petits fours that will be the mark of a gracious hostess.

19-oz. box $5.95

Maison Glass

Christmas Petits Fours

The prettiest, daintiest, and most exquisitely flavored continental cake confections ever tasted are these tiny cakelets with rich butter-cream filling. Many flavors, enrobed in dark and light chocolate.

36 petits fours $4.95
72 petits fours $9.95

The Swiss Colony

French Petits Fours

Prepared in the traditional French way with layers of dainty cake and rich, creamy filling, these keep fresh for weeks in the refrigerator, or for many months in the freezer.

32 petits fours $5.50

Figi's

Petits Fours 'n Tortes

There are 21 varieties of petits fours and tiny tortes: rum, mint, Dobosh tortes; orange, pineapple, toffee, lemon, almond, strawberry petits fours; Dobosh, mint, almond, pecan, pistachio, walnut fudge creams; and cherry, Crème de Cacao, apricot, orange, brandy, rum cordials.

96 petits fours $12.95

The Swiss Colony

Roulade

Freshly ground walnuts or poppyseeds are wrapped in a light, flaky dough that is a melt-in-your-mouth mixture. Only pure natural ingredients are used, and the result is all golden brown goodness. When kept in the refrigerator this roulade will stay fresh indefinitely. Specify walnut or poppyseed filling.

approx 1 lb. $6.98
3 lb. $19.00
5 lb. $36.00

Paprikas Weiss

Strudel

Here's a Hungarian confection that is a fine, flaky pastry wrapped around a mouth-watering filling of poppy or fruit or nuts or cheese or cabbage. Take your pick of fillings—or a selection of all.

1-lb. strip $9.98
3-lb. strip $28.00
6-lb. strip $54.00

Paprikas Weiss

Danish Strudels

This is the traditional strudel made slightly less sweet and a little thinner. Light flaky pastry dough outside plus a scrumptious apple/apricot filling and the crunch of walnuts within. No preservatives added.

2 9-oz. strudels $6.95

Pepperidge Farm

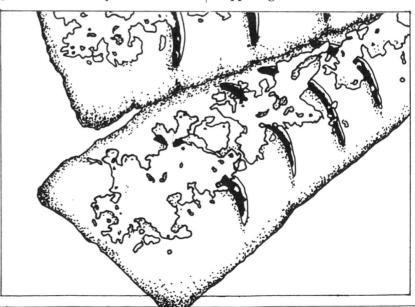

Strudels and Tortes

Strudels — Apple, Cherry, Nut Mohn, Kraut:

	½ strip	1 strip
Regular	$2.00	$3.90
Cheese	2.00	4.00
Special (with extra filling)		5.25

Tortes:	6-inch	8-inch	10-inch
Chestnut	$5.95	$11.75	$16.95
Chocolate	3.95	7.30	11.95
Dobos		7.30	11.95
Mocha Nut	3.95	7.30	11.95
Pishinger		7.75	12.45
Rigo-Black Forest		11.25	13.95
Rum		7.30	11.95
Sacher		7.30	11.95

Mrs. Herbst Pastry & Strudel

Viennese Kipferli

These popular crescents are as light as a sugar-spun cloud and delicately flavored with vanilla. A classic accompaniment to good coffee and conversation.

7-oz. box $2.98
3 boxes $8.00
6 boxes $14.00
12 boxes $25.00

Paprikas Weiss

Almond Paste

Almond paste may be frozen for long storing; with the small can, you can use the entire contents when you open it. Paste is made of pure, blanched selected almonds and sugar and comes with delicious recipes for marzipan, almond cake filling, and macaroons.

8-oz. can $1.65
7-lb. can $17.50

Maid of Scandinavia

Chestnut Spread (Purée de Marrons)

"Gesztenye Purée Haszalatra Kerzen" are chestnuts with sugar and vanilla. They are an instant dessert—no cooking. Just mix with cream for a delicious sauce or use as a topping.

8-oz. can $1.98
1-lb. 15-oz. can $4.75

Lekvar By The Barrel

Macaroon Paste

For making all types of almond tarts, macaroons, Danish fillings, and marzipan confections, macaroon paste may be used wherever almond paste is specified.

1-lb. can $1.95
7-lb. can $12.50

Maid of Scandinavia

Poppy Seed

Imported poppy seed, freshly ground and sifted.

1 lb. $2.49

Lekvar By The Barrel

Poppy Seed Filling

Many of the most loved recipes from Europe call for a poppy seed filling. This one comes packed in vacuum-sealed cans for freshness. Directions are on the can.

7½ lb. $9.95

Maid of Scandinavia

Prune Lekvar

A very thick puree of plump sweet prunes makes a mouth-watering filling for cakes and pastries. It keeps its smooth texture throughout the baking process and will not melt or run.

1 lb. $1.59
8½-lb. can $8.75

Lekvar By The Barrel

Strudel Dough

Real Hungarian Strudel Dough, the ''jewel of desserts,'' comes ready to use in a package of four sheets. Instructions are included. Write the supplier for current prices.

Lekvar By The Barrel

Aplets, Cotlets, Grapelets

A Turkish delight is made with the fresh fruits grown at the foot of the rugged Cascade Mountains in Washington. The candies are a unique blend of apples, apricots, grapes, and walnuts and have a personality all their own. Each piece is guaranteed not to conform to any other, but each maintains the same high quality of texture and taste.

3 5-oz. packages $5.00
Family pack (13 oz.) $4.00

Calico Kitchen

Benne Candy

A sweet, brittlelike candy chock full of Benne—those rich, spicy, honey-colored ''good luck'' seeds. Candy is packed in heavy transparent-plastic boxes with its tangy freshness sealed in.

7-oz. box $3.90

Byrd Cookie Co.

2.

Candies

Amaretti

These are Italian macaroons. Served with caffè espresso, they are a perfect ending to a festive meal. Sweet, but dry, crisp, and airy.

8 oz. $3.10
1 lb. $5.50
5 lb. $21.50
1 lb. $2.40

Manganaro Foods

Bailey's Assortments

Bailey's has long been a landmark in Boston, and famous for the high quality of its candies. All candy is handmade in small batches daily. The store sells chocolate, wrapped caramels, mints, nuts and nut pieces, jellies, hard candies, and the Bailey traditions: crystallized ginger, Bailey kisses (caramel-covered marshmallows), coconut cakes, and molasses coconut cakes. Here are some suggested assortments.

Fireside Selection	1, 2, 3, 5 lb.	$3.25 per lb.
The Holiday Box	1, 2, 3, 5 lb.	2.75 per lb.
Liberty Bell Box	9 oz.	1.65
Wedgewood Package	12 oz.	2.50

Bailey's

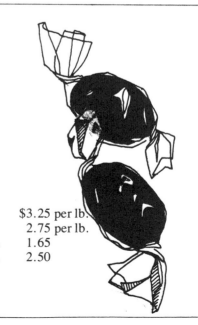

Bissinger's Assortments

Bissinger's manufactures several chocolate assortments in one- to five-pound boxes: hard candies, taffy, and chocolate balls wrapped in foil. There are many suitable gifts and holiday-packaged assortments from $6.95 to $19.95. Here are two popular selections:

Bissinger's Famous Assortment—all their chocolates—nut centers, cream centers, fruits, crips, chewies $4.95 per lb.
Empress Eugénie Selection—a wide variety with greater concentration on nut balls, silistrias, and other popular pieces $5.50 per lb.

Bissinger's

Brandied Cherries

These are the Fabbri brand from Italy. Cherries come packed in a fancy bottle.

Net wt. 23 oz. $8.55

Le Jardin du Gourmet

Carob Pecans

These are for people who like the taste of chocolate but wish to avoid it. The carob pod, a native of the Mediterranean, has the flavor and sweetness of chocolate but is not chocolate. Carob Pecans are a natural mixture of pecans and a rich coating that contains carob powder, molasses, wheat germ, and rose hips.

7-oz. box
   1 to 29 boxes $1.75 each
   1 to 4 cases (30 boxes per case)
    $45.00 each
1-lb. 11-oz. enameled tin
   1 to 11 tins $6.45 each
   1 to 4 cases (12 tins per case)
    $64.80 each

Koinonia Products

Chocolate Cordials

From Austria come 20 of the most delicious cordials. The rich chocolate is molded into miniature bottles that hold a refreshing selection of flavors: cherry, black currant, raspberry, strawberry and apricot. In gold box.

Net wt. 12 oz. $4.75

The Swiss Colony

Chocolate Pecan Fudge

Delicious creamy-style fudge with choice pecans comes packed in an attractive gift tin.

Net wt. 1¾ lb. $3.95

The Swiss Colony

Chocolate Tower

Pastries and chocolates tied with bright red ribbon and topped with a bow make this Chocolate Tower. Includes 15 beautifully decorated fudge creams; 2¾-oz. Almond & Dobosh tortes; 4-oz. macadamia nut chocolates; 5 oz. Heavenly Hash; 4 oz. of fine assorted chocolate candy.

1 tower $9.95

The Swiss Colony

Chocolatier

Attention, chocolate lovers! Here are three divine pecan delights and one divine divinity. A Chocolatier

includes toasted pecan halves covered with rich chocolate, choco-caramel pecan clusters, and creamy home-style fudge filled with small pecan pieces. A light and airy pecan divinity completes the treat.

2-lb. 9-oz. box $9.50
Case of 5 shipped to one address
   $42.50

Sunnyland Farms

Choco-Nuts

Fancy pecan halves are roasted and salted, then individually "enrobed" in a delicious creamy milk chocolate. A "yummy" favorite of many. They come in a gift box or in a homey tin for everyday use.

17-oz. Gift Box $6.50
2¼-lb. Jumble Pack $9.50

Sunnyland Farms

Divinity

Exceptionally good pecan divinity that is also exceptionally light and fluffy. It is dropped, not cut, in order to seal in its kitchen freshness and flavor.

Net wt. 1 lb. $5.15

Priester's Pecans

Fauchon Assortments

To receive candy from Fauchon in Paris is considered the MOST! Fauchon is world famous for many items, but for most of its customers—and the list includes kings, movie stars, and just plain chocolate lovers—it is revered for its chocolate.

Boite "Civa" (Assorted French Chocolate Delicacies):
Round:

0.850 kg (approx. 1.9 lb.)	$42.00
1.100 kg (approx. 2.4 lb.)	58.00
1.600 kg (approx. 3.5 lb.)	70.00
4.000 kg (approx. 8.8 lb.)	130.00

Rectangular (large size):

1.100 kg (approx. 2.4 lb.)	$42.00
1.450 kg (approx. 3.2 lb.)	60.00
2.300 kg (approx. 5.1 lb.)	77.00
3.900 kg (approx. 8.6 lb.)	130.00

Rectangular (small size):

0.700 kg (approx. 1.5 lb.)	$48.00
0.900 kg (approx. 2 lb.)	50.00
1.450 kg (approx. 3.2 lb.)	62.00

Fauchon

Fondant

Fondant is the base for so many types of candies. It is almost essential for icing petits fours; or you can pour it over cakes, cast it into molds, and so forth. All you need to do is heat, color, and flavor it. White.

2½ lb. $3.50

Maid of Scandinavia

Fruit Thins

Slim squares of fresh fruit candies make a real Hawaiian treat. Mandarin-mint, passion fruit, guava, pineapple, toasted coconut.

30 oz. $6.95 postpaid in U.S.

Kemoo Farm Foods

Fudge Ring

Rich, creamy, loaded with pecans, then formed into a holiday ring. Covered with rich pure chocolate and choice pecan halves. Comes in a gift tin.

2½ lb. $7.45

The Swiss Colony

Gianduiotti

A smooth blend of milk chocolate and ground Italian hazelnuts. Little triangles individually wrapped in gold foil. Available in Motta or Perugina brand; the price is the same for either one.

8 oz. $3.25
1 lb. $5.95

Manganaro Foods

Ginger

Fortnum & Mason offers an exotic assortment of Crown Devon, Royal Winton, and Coalport jars as containers for their super-quality gingers. A sample:

Crown Devon "Lowestoft" jar with 2 lb. F & M young stem ginger $23.00. Postage and packing $4.00
Crown Devon "Posy" jar with 6 oz. young stem ginger $7.00. Postage and packing $2.00
Old Foley "Chinese Rose" jar with 2 lb. F & M young stem ginger $23.00. Postage and packing $4.00
Royal Winton "Fruit" design storage jar containing 16 oz. F & M crystallized ginger $8.00. Postage and packing $2.00

Fortnum & Mason

Godiva

Made from Belgian chocolatier recipes with no artificial flavorings or preservatives. The distinctive golden ballotin contains light and dark chocolates filled with mousse, mocha, praline, cream, and much more.

½ lb. $4.95
1 lb. $8.95
2 lb. $16.95
3 lb. $23.95

Pepperidge Farm

Green Mint Straws

Crisp mint centers with green coating that are as pleasing to the eye as to the taste. A mint delight!

1-lb. box $4.00
2-lb. box $7.50

Kate Latter's

Kentucky Cream Pull

Delightfully light and fluffy vanilla-flavored and uncoated creams make this delicious and unusual candy literally melt in your mouth. Made from whole milk, light cream, whipping cream, and sugar. Chocolate-covered creams are coated with unsweetened chocolate liqueur. Unlike any other candy in your experience!

13-oz. box $3.20

Rebecca-Ruth Candy

Pure Maple Sugar Bon Bons

Each of these melt-in-your-mouth candies is in a different and fancy shape. Makes a delicious and attractive package.

12 oz. $4.50. Postage and packing $1.00

Sugarbush Farm

Marzipan Bars

Chocolate-covered Marzipan Bars are delightful little loaves of flavorful marzipan dipped in rich bittersweet chocolate and elegantly wrapped in gleaming red foil to keep them as fresh as the day they were made.

1½-oz. loaves 4 for $4.98
Box of 24 1½-oz. loaves $25.00
3-oz. loaves 3 for $4.98
Box of 12 3-oz. loaves $18.00

Paprikas Weiss

Marzipan Baskets

Fresh Marzipan Baskets that look like they came straight from the grocer's. Mouth-watering marzipan in assorted fruit, vegetable, and plump strawberry shapes. Authentically colored and in genuine fruit baskets.

1 basket $1.98
3 baskets $5.00

Paprikas Weiss

Established 1928
CANDY AND GIFT SHOP
300 Royal Street
New Orleans, La. 70130

The Mail-Order Food Book

Miniatures

Catherine has been famous for years for its hand-dipped chocolates. It sells the popular bite-size miniatures (average 60–70 pieces per pound) made from tradition-tested recipes. House specialties include Pecan Roll; Carmel and Nougat; Pecan Mallows; White, Bittersweet, or Milk Chocolate; and Butter Krunch, a butter-nut brittle covered in chocolate and rolled in ground nuts.

Berkshire Assortment:	1 lb.	$3.50
	2 lb.	$7.00
	4 lb.	$14.00
Assorted Nuts:	1 lb.	$3.75
	2 lb.	$7.50
	4 lb.	$15.00
Yankee Nut and Fruit Assortment:	1 lb.	$3.75
	2 lb.	$7.50
	4 lb.	$15.00

Catherine's Chocolate Shoppe

The Mint Kentucky Colonels

Mild-flavored mint centers surrounded by two luscious pecan halves sautéed in butter and salted. This delicious center is then dipped in thin rich chocolate to become a gourmet's delight.

13-oz. box $4.20

Rebecca-Ruth Candy

Pecan Bark

A really fine candy loaded with crunchy top-quality pecans. It comes in five delicious, different flavors—milk chocolate, white chocolate, bittersweet chocolate, butterscotch, and peppermint. You'll want to have a tin of each for good nibbling at holiday parties, but it's a difficult choice to make.

1-lb. 11-oz. tin, any flavor $6.95

Sunnyland Farms

Toasted Pecan Brittle

This crunchy toasted Pecan Brittle is made in Priester's confectionary kitchen. This treat is full of meaty pecans combined with the highest-quality ingredients and cooked in small batches to retain the delicious homemade flavor. Packaged in an attractive tin.

Net wt. 1 lb. $5.60
Case of 12 tins shipped to one address $53.35

Priester's Pecans

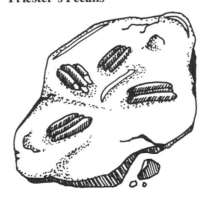

Pecan Clusters

This old favorite still tops lots of lists. Made of crisp big pecan pieces smothered with thick creamy caramel and covered with a layer of rich milk chocolate. This has been one of the most popular pecan candies ever since it was first created some thirty years ago.

1-lb. Gift Tin $6.30
3½-lb. Home Box $14.35
Case of 9 Gift Tins shipped to one address $45.25

Sunnyland Farms

Pecan Dates

The natural goodness of the finest dates and nuts offered by Mother Earth, moist California Deglet Noor dates are stuffed with a plump Georgia pecan half. No sugar and no frosting, so they are excellent for sugar-free dieters.

12-oz. box
   1 to 29 boxes $2.15 each
   1 to 4 cases (30 boxes per case) $58.50 each
2¼-lb. enameled tin
   1 to 11 tins $6.95
   1 to 4 cases (12 tins per case) $75.00 each

Koinonia Products

Pecan Logs

A yummy log to be sliced and served as delicious morsels. Each log has a center of creamy nougat filling coated with a thick layer of delicious caramel that has been rolled in fresh crunchy pecans. The logs are uneven in size because each one is handmade in the Sunnyland kitchen.

Gift Box (3 7-oz. logs) $5.50
Home Box (4 12-oz. logs) $9.20
Case of 8 Gift Boxes shipped to one address $35.00

Sunnyland Farms

Candied Pecan Halves

Sugar and Spiced candied halves are big, firm pecan halves that have been dipped in pure syrup to which has been added a special blend of cinnamon, allspice, and clove. The sugar sweetness and tangy spices meld with the unique taste that you get only from a good pecan.

Orange Frosted pecan halves are cooked in a syrup containing real orange juice. This is a scrumptious confection that you will hardly believe.

Sugar and Spiced
2-lb. Gift Box	$ 7.90
3-lb. Economy Pack	10.00
6 14-oz. Poly Packs	16.85
Case of 4 shipped to one address	24.40

Orange Frosted
2-lb Gift Box	$ 8.15
3-lb. Economy Pack	10.65
6 14-oz. Poly Packs	17.40
Case of 4 shipped to one address	29.10

Half 'n Half (Orange Frosted and Sugar and Spiced)
2-lb. Gift Box	$ 8.25
Case of 4 shipped to one address	28.80
Case of 10 shipped to one address	71.40

Sunnyland Farms

More Pecan Logs

Made from a specially formulated recipe—the velvet-smooth nougat center is sprinkled with colorful red cherries and hand-dipped in whole cream caramel—then rolled in pecan kernels. They'll arrive in four cellophane-wrapped logs for individual eating; or they may be sliced for serving.

Net wt. 1½ lb. $6.85

Priester's Pecans

Jane's Pecan Pralines

These big cartwheels made from a newly perfected recipe are loaded with as many big Sunnyland pieces as they will hold. Made fresh to order, each one by hand, they are a mouth-watering treat.

Home Box (nine pralines 1½ to 2 oz. each) $5.55
Jumbo Box (20 pralines) $9.10

Sunnyland Farms

Priester's Pecan Pralines

Rich, creamy pralines chock full of fresh tasty pecans are made from a treasured Creole recipe developed to its present superb goodness by Priester's.

Net wt. 1 lb. $5.50

Priester's Pecans

Pralines

These are Kate Latter's famous original New Orleans Creole Pralines. Made from rich Louisiana plantation cane sugar and chunky pecans. They come in a variety of flavors; and they come either creamy or chewy.

Famous New Orleans Creole Pralines—individually wrapped and in a colorful souvenir mailing carton. 1 dozen $4.50. 2 dozen $8.00

Pralines in Souvenir Cotton Bale—12 pralines packed individually and available in assorted flavors—rum, chocolate, maple, vanilla, chewy, and original. Also packed in individual flavor of your choice. $5.50

Creamy Pecan Pralines—large pralines chock full of Louisiana pecans and pure cream. 1 dozen $4.50. 2 dozen $8.00

Assorted Pecan Pralines—creamy

assortment of three flavors. Choose from vanilla, rum, chocolate, and maple pralines. 1 dozen $4.50. 2 dozen $8.00

Chewy Pecan Pralines—made with caramel cream and pecans—delightfully chewy. 1 dozen $4.50. 2 dozen $8.00

Southern Assortment—includes chewy pralines, creamy pralines, pecan rolls, and divinity fudge. 1 dozen $4.50. 2 dozen $8.00

Kate Latter's Special Assortment—24 delicious assorted pralines—4 each of creole, creamy, maple, chewy, chocolate, and rum. $8.00

Pecan Chews—creamy caramel and pecans coated in luscious chocolate and made in the shape of turtles. 1 lb. $5.00. 2 lb. $8.50

Kate Latter's

Perugina Assortments

Perugina of Italy sells a rich
assortment of beautifully wrapped
chocolates.

Baci, or "Kisses"—a dreamy bittersweet chocolate
kiss with chopped hazelnuts.   5 pieces $1.25. Postage and packing $1.25
10 pieces $2.50. Postage and packing $1.50
32 pieces $7.50. Postage and packing $1.95

Tenda Oro—a rich variety of elegantly wrapped
solid and creamy chocolate centers.
1 lb. 1½ oz. $9.95. Postage and packing $2.35
1 lb. 7 oz. $14.95. Postage and packing $2.50
1 lb. 13 oz. $16.95. Postage and packing $2.50

Torrone—the famous Italian Nougat candy. 1 box (18 pieces) $3.75. Postage and packing $1.75

Perugina of Italy

Plumbridge Assortments

Plumbridge is neither a store nor a shop, but an "establishment" located in the former townhouse of Oleg Cassini. Nowhere outside the establishment does a sign indicate that candy is sold on the premises, but for nearly a century it has been the confectionary establishment for the most affluent. Its candy packaging is so distinctive that it is seen in *House & Garden, Gourmet,* and *Harper's Bazaar.* Plumbridge has no paid advertising but manages to flourish on word-of-mouth recommendations.

Plumbridge sells no milk chocolate, only a dark semisweet chocolate cooked on kitchen stoves and poured on marble slabs to cool. Prices are definitely in the high category, but no more than is to be expected for an "establishment."

Assorted chocolates—caramel, mint, nut patties, coconut, butter crunch 1 lb. $7.50
Carriage Trade Favorites
   The Hansom: chocolate, fruit, pecans   1 box $16.00
   The Stanhope: chocolate, fruit, pecans, mocha nuts   1 box $22.50

Plumbridge

Rebecca-Ruth Candy

Homemade candy is alive and well—at least in Frankfort, Kentucky. "Miss Boo," as she is known far and wide, is the proprietor of the Rebecca-Ruth kitchens there. Her stove turns out an assortment of delectable confections that, because they are made of pure ingredients, must be kept refrigerated. One "pure ingredient" is genuine Kentucky bourbon; unfortunately, candy made with it cannot be sold outside the state of Kentucky. However, a wide variety of other delights have pleased candy lovers around the country.

Americana Chocolates—14 different and delicious centers each dipped in a rich coating of dark chocolate. Centers of brown sugar, black walnut fudge, crème de menthe and rum, black walnut-butter brittle, coconut cream, almond paste with candied cherry, almond paste and fondant layers topped with pecan half, coffee cream topped by sautéed salted pecan, rich caramel centers. cream pulled candy, chocolate and vanilla butter creams, and chocolate fudge nut ball. This is truly an elegant assortment. Recommended by Craig Claiborne of the *New York Times.* 13-oz. box $4.45.

Opera Creams—a time-honored favorite of rich vanilla centers made with dairy-rich milk and cream and pure vanilla extract. Each luscious cream center is dipped and covered with a thin, rich dark-chocolate coating. Opera creams are an elegant delight that will accentuate any gathering. 13-oz. box $2.95

R and M Chocolates—a delectable assortment of rum and crème de menthe chocolates. Soft rum and butter centers topped with a luscious pecan half, and luscious mild mint and pecan centers topped with a salted pecan half and covered with a thin layer of rich dark chocolate. 13-oz. box $3.95

Rebecca-Ruth Candy

Rum Chocolates

For the connoisseur. The box contains soft rum-butter centers topped with a luscious pecan half. This delicious center is then covered with a rich, dark-chocolate coating. The robust rum flavoring is a delightfully different taste treat. Recommended by *Gourmet* magazine.

13-oz. box $3.95

Rebecca-Ruth Candy

The Mail-Order Food Book

Southern Colonels

Hand-dipped chocolates that bring back memories of grandmother's confections. These are fresh pecan kernels covered with whole-cream caramel and hand-dipped in the finest dark and milk chocolates. Order these from October through May; they are not recommended for summer shipment.

Net wt. 1 lb. 4 oz. $6.95

Priester's Pecans

Southern Hospitality

Warmhearted hospitality is adequately expressed in this gift of handcrafted pecan treats. Their good old-fashioned flavor is supreme. And the selection contains all the old-time favorites: 8 oz. Pecan Date Rolls; 12 oz. Pecan Bark; 1 lb. Chocolate Toasted Pecans; 1 lb. Chocolate Pecan Fudge and Pecan Divinity; 8 oz. Frosted Pecan Kernels; 8 oz. Orange Pecan Kernels; 8 oz. Roasted-Salted Pecan Halves; 8 oz. Pecan Fiddle Sticks; 6 oz. Pecan Log.

Assortment above $23.15

Priester's Pecans

Sugarplums

Heavenly nougats of crisp English walnuts, zingy apricots, and plump, sweet Medjool dates finely chopped and combined just so, then

dipped—half of them into creamy milk chocolate, and half into an extra-rich dark chocolate. Over a pound. Comes in a fancy gift box.

Order gift number 350
Weight 3 lbs. 3 oz. $8.45, delivered

Harry and David

Farrah's Original Harrogate Toffee

An old-fashioned toffee of absolute purity made with butter and sugar. "Crescent" tin contains Harrogate Toffee in small wrapped pieces.

12-oz. tin $6.00

Egertons

Torrone

A fancy Italian nougat made with roasted hazelnuts, almonds, sugar, and honey. Box of 18 individual torrone chunks in a variety of flavors in fancy wrappings. Each box decorated with a reproduction of a noted Italian scene. Available in Motta or Perugina brand; the price is the same for either one.

Box (18 chunks) $3.40

Manganaro Foods

3.

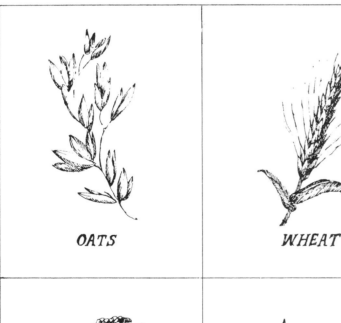

OATS

WHEAT

BUCKWHEAT

RYE

Cornucopia Cereal

A nutritious natural cereal made in small batches from rolled oats, plump Monukka raisins, chopped almonds, dried apricots, sunflower seeds, dried apples, and powdered whole oranges. Bagged in old-fashioned coffee bags. Cornucopia can also be baked into delicious cookies; a recipe is included in each order. There is no raw sugar, and no artificial sweeteners or preservatives are added.

13-oz. bag $1.65 all areas
3-lb. bag $4.75, $5.00, $5.50.
(Prices vary according to delivery area.)

The Appleyard Corporation

Pecan-Peanut Granola

This granola makes a nutritious breakfast or snacking event. It is made from wheat, oats, and soy flakes with gobs of pecans and peanuts roasted together in vegetable oil, honey, and sugar. Add your own favorite canned, dried, or fresh fruit, sweetener, and milk. You'll come back for more.

1-lb. cello bags
   1–9 bags $1.55
   10–23 bags $1.45
   1–4 cases (24 bags per case)
    $33.60
1-lb. 11-oz. enameled tins
   1-11 tins $3.85
   1–4 cases (12 tins per case) $38.40

Koinonia Products

FLOURS

Flour is made by grinding wheat or other grains. Wheat flour is the most common kind, and in the United States the word *flour* usually means wheat flour. Other flours include rye flour, barley flour, oat flour, and corn flour.

Flour can be classified as simply flour or as enriched flour, self-rising flour, phosphated flour, bromated flour, or whole wheat flour. The first five are white flours and are often called ''patent'' flours. Any of these flours may be made from hard wheats or soft wheats. Flours made from hard wheats are used chiefly to make bread, while flours made from soft wheats are used mainly to make biscuits, cakes, pastries, and crackers.

Whole wheat flour contains all the parts of the wheat kernel, including the branny coats and the germ as well as the inner portion from which white flour is made. Whole wheat flour is also called ''entire'' wheat flour. It used to be called ''graham'' flour, after a man named Sylvester Graham, who preferred this kind of flour and thought everyone should use it. Whole wheat flour is still listed as ''graham'' flour in some catalogues.

Arrowhead Mills Flours

	Sacks	Price
Buckwheat Flour	12 2-lb.	$12.50
Pastry Flour	10 5-lb.	16.40
Pastry Flour	12 2-lb.	8.80
Rice Flour	12 2-lb.	14.30
Rye Flour	12 2-lb.	6.80
Soy Flour	12 1½-lb.	6.60
Triticale Flour	12 2-lb.	6.50

Arrowhead Mills

Byrd Flours

	Sacks	Price
Brown Rice Flour	2 lb.	$2.15
	5 lb.	4.20
Buckwheat Flour	2 lb.	2.15
	5 lb.	4.25
Oat Flour	2 lb.	2.15
	5 lb.	4.25
Soy Flour	2 lb.	2.15
	5 lb.	4.25
Unbleached Flour	2 lb.	2.15
(wheat germ added)	5 lb.	4.25
Whole Wheat (Graham)	2 lb.	2.15
Flour	5 lb.	4.25

Byrd Mill Co.

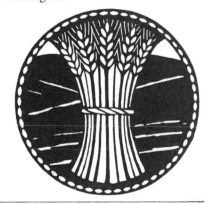

Birkett Mills Flours

	Sacks	Price
Bessie Unbleached Stone Ground Pastry Flour (for cakes, pies, and cookies)	5 lb.	$ .80
Birkett's Stone Ground Graham Flour	5 lb.	1.00
Larrowe's Old Fashioned Stone Ground Pure Buckwheat Flour (light or dark)	2½ lb.	.95
	5 lb.	1.50
Wolff's Stone Ground 100% Whole Rye Flour	2 lb.	.60
Wolff's Stone Ground 100% Whole Wheat Flour	2 lb.	.60

Birkett Mills

Erewhon Flours

	Quantity and Sack Size	Unit Price	Price
Brown Rice Flour	12 2-lb.	$1.20	$14.40
Buckwheat Flour (dark)	12 2-lb.	1.03	12.36
Hard Red Winter Whole Wheat Flour (Deaf Smith brand)	12 2-lb.	.55	6.80
Rye Flour	12 2-lb.	.59	7.08
Soft Winter Whole Wheat Flour (Deaf Smith brand)	12 2-lb.	.73	8.76
Triticale Flour	12 2-lb.	.58	6.96
White Corn Meal	12 2-lb.	.64	7.68
Yellow Corn Meal	12 2-lb.	.54	6.48

Erewhon

Infinity Flours

	Quantity and Sack Size	Unit Price	Price
Barley Flour	12 1-lb.	$ .52	$ 6.24
Corn Flour	12 1-lb.	.30	3.60
White Flour (organic)	12 2-lb.	.68	8.16
White Flour (unbleached)	50 lb.	.265	13.25
Whole Wheat Flour (pastry)	12 2-lb.	.68	8.16
Whole Wheat Flour (stoneground, organic)	6 5-lb.	1.36	8.16
Whole Wheat Flour (organic)	6 5-lb.	1.50	9.00

Infinity Foods

Nature Plus Flours

	Sacks	Price
Elam's 3-1 Flour	2 lb.	$.89
Fearn Bran Muffin Flour	1 lb.	.45
Fearn Corn Muffin Flour	1 lb.	.45
Fearn Unbleached White Flour	1 lb.	.49
Fearn Whole Wheat Flour	1 lb.	.41
Old Stone Mill Whole Wheat Flour	2 lb.	.75

Nature Plus

MIXES

Country Mixes

These mixes are new and complete; you need only add water. They are perfect for everyone who loves flaky biscuits, light pancakes, and old-fashioned spoonbread. The Country Mix pack contains a one-pound bag each of Southern-style Spoonbread, Biscuit Mix, Pancake Mix, and Whole Wheat Pancake Mix.

4 1-lb. bags $4.70–$5.65 depending on delivery area.

Broadbent B&B Food Products

Granola Bread Mix

This makes the nuttiest, yummiest bread. The mix is combined with dissolved yeast, and with the usual rising, punching down, dividing, and panning, makes four loaves. No preservatives added.

4 lb. $2.95

Maid of Scandinavia

Country Store Pancake Mix

Here's an old-fashioned mix that is light and fluffy with a flavor that is super. It comes in buckwheat or buttermilk (both cost the same) so the choice is difficult.

2-lb. bag $2.75 to $3.15 depending on delivery area.

Green Mountain Sugar House

5 Flour Stoneground Pancake Mix

This is a delicious and nutritious whole-grain pancake mix that is made from wheat, rye, buckwheat, soy, and corn. Once you try it you'll love it.

2-lb. bag $2.10, $2.30, or $2.75 depending on delivery area.

The Appleyard Corporation

Pastry Mix

Just add water, and depending on the type of rolls or pastry, add also yeast, eggs, perhaps shortening, to make sweet rolls or puffy Danish quickly and easily. Special recipes are included.

2 lb. $1.45

Maid of Scandinavia

Potato Dumpling Mix

The famous ''Panni'' does all the work. No peeling, no grating, no pressing—just add water and get 10 to 15 fluffy dumplings.

8-oz. box $1.25
12 boxes $14.00
24 boxes $27.00

Paprikas Weiss

Potato Pancake Mix

The famous ''Panni'' does all the work. Just open the package and add water—it's as easy as that to make 25 delicious crisp potato pancakes.

8-oz. box $1.25
12 boxes $14.00
24 boxes $27.00

Paprikas Weiss

SOURDOUGH

Sourdough

Steeped in the romance of the West and the great outdoors, sourdough has come indoors. It is now found in millions of kitchens across the United States and Canada. Sourdough Jack's starter packages (complete with instructions) are direct descendants of the starter Sourdough Jack brought down from Alaska a quarter of a century ago. Treated with care, a starter will last as long as its parent

and give you a lifetime of baking. Fill your kitchen with the heady, tantalizing fragrance of hot sourdough breads and other tempting foodstuffs.

	Each	Cost per 2
Sourdough starter	$1.75	$ 2.75
Cookery Book	3.80	6.75
Book-Starter Set	4.70	8.15
Gift Pack	7.50	13.00

Sourdough Jack's

Sourdough Bread

Different, delicious San Francisco sourdough bread can be baked and shipped fresh to you in any shape (round or long) you wish. A year-round bread subscription is a perfect gourmet gift. Just set the date—beginning, middle, or end of month—and delivery is guaranteed.

Year-round: $38.00 Western U.S.
$61.00 Central U.S.
$50.00 Eastern U.S.
Single orders:

Number of Loaves	Western U.S.
2	$ 3.29
4	5.10
6	7.10
12	13.00

Eastern U.S.	Central U.S.
$ 4.29	$ 5.19
6.69	7.89
9.59	10.99
17.79	19.79

Calico Kitchens

North Beach Picnic Bread

Two 1-pound loaves of famous round San Francisco sourdough bread with a 1-pound wheel of creamy Monterey Jack cheese, a 1-pound stick of dry San Francisco Italian salami, a bleached hardwood bread board, and an 8-inch blade British Lamson stainless-steel bread knife are tucked into a genuine French string bag for many years of happy picnicking.

As above $18.00 Western U.S.
$21.00 Eastern U.S.

Calico Kitchens

French Latic Sourdough Starter

This can be used in making those delicious crusty loaves of French sourdough breads. Or it makes hotcakes that are light as a feather; biscuits that melt in your mouth. Comes with directions and recipes.

1 jar $2.00

Nichols Garden Nursery

Oregon Pioneer Sourdough Starter

This is the same "starter" used by the early Oregon pioneers in their lusty baking in the 1850s. It is claimed that this is the starter that was taken to Alaska in the Gold Rush of 1889 and became the basis of the legendary sourdough starters of that country. Comes with directions for preparing and recipes.

1 jar $2.00

Nichols Garden Nursery

WHOLE GRAINS

Arrowhead Whole Grains

	12 2-lb. bags
Barley	$ 9.80
Long Grain Brown Rice	13.80
Medium Grain Brown Rice	13.80
Popcorn	8.70
Short Grain Rice	13.80
Toasted Buckwheat	15.90
Whole Grain Berries	5.30
Whole Grain Rye	5.40
Whole Millet	8.50

Arrowhead Mills

Bulgur

When the Turks say "pilaf" they mean the real hearty variety made with flavorful bulgur wheat. This bulgur is the original ingredient. Serve with shish kebab or any other meat dish.

16-oz. pkg. $2.59
3 pkg. $7.50
6 pkg. $14.00
12 pkg. $26.00

Paprikas Weiss

Byrd Whole Grains

Grinding whole kernels of grain between stones to make meal and flour is an ancient art. The refined version of meals and flours is relatively new and is the result of mass production. The only way to retain natural flavors, nutritional values, and vitamins in the grains is to process them slowly, without heat—the way it is done at Byrd Mill.

Byrd Mill began in 1740. Young Patrick Henry often brought corn, wheat, and buckwheat from his father's nearby plantation to Byrd Mill. It continued in operation at its original site until 1968 when an untimely fire brought an end to production in the original building. But the famous Byrd method of grinding flours and meals has survived.

	East of the Mississippi		West of the Mississippi	
	2 lb.	5 lb.	2 lb.	5 lb.
Buckwheat Flour	$2.15	$4.20	$2.45	$4.95
Cracked Wheat Cereal	2.15	4.25	2.45	4.95
Fox Hunters Meal	2.15	4.25	2.45	4.95
Natural Unbleached Flour	2.15	4.25	2.45	4.95
Old Tyme Yellow Grits	2.15	4.25	2.45	4.95
White Rice Flour	2.15	4.25	2.45	4.95

Byrd Mill Co.

Infinity Whole Grains

Buckwheat (raw)	12 1-lb.	$6.80
Buckwheat (roasted)	12 1-lb.	6.95
Bulgur Wheat	12 1-lb.	6.84
Cous Cous (Zakia brand)	55 lb.	$45.10

Infinity Foods

Erewhon Whole Grains

	Quantity and Size	Price
Barley, pearled, unfumigated (Eden brand)	12 1-lb.	$ 4.29
(A.M. brand)	12 2-lb.	10.08
Buckwheat, whole toasted, brown, hulled kasha		
(Eden brand)	12 12-oz.	5.88
Millet (Eden brand)	12 1-lb.	4.44
(A.M. brand)	12 2-lb.	8.76
Popcorn (Eden brand)	12 1-lb.	5.88
Rye (A.M. brand)	12 2-lb.	6.00
Wheat, hard red winter (Deaf Smith brand)	12 1-lb.	3.48

Erewhon

Nature Plus Whole Grains

(Prices for 24-lb. bag)

Barley	$25.00
Buckwheat Grits	29.00
Buckwheat Groat (raw)	29.00
Buckwheat Groat (roasted)	29.00
Bulgur (parched wheat)	27.00
Cut Oats	23.00
Millet	29.00
Poppyseed	79.00
Rolled Oats	25.00
Scotch Oats (Elam's brand)	27.00
Wild Rice 4 oz.	1.99
1 lb.	7.50

Nature Plus

4.

Cheese, Pasta, and Wild Rice

Biergarten

A pungent, soft-textured cheese with small "eyes" and pale golden coloring. Always foil-wrapped to protect its delicate ripeness, Biergarten is at its best when served with sliced pumpernickel or rye bread, topped with an onion.

2½ lb. $6.75

The Swiss Colony

Blue Cheese

A blue-veined cheese similar in flavor and texture to its foreign cousin, Roquefort. Crumbled in French dressing, it imparts a unique flavor to salads. Not available during June, July, or August.

Net wt. over 2½ lb. $8.25
Whole wheel (net wt. over 6 lb.)
$16.95

The Swiss Cheese Shop

CHEESE

More Blue Cheese

Rich and ravishing, blue-marbled and crumbly. Glorious in salads, for canapés, table use, and dessert.

1¼ lb. $3.95

The Swiss Colony

Oregon Blue Cheese Wheel

Made from a traditional Danish formula that gives it a superb, velvety texture with a full, hearty creamy flavor, this cheese has been allowed to ripen slowly to develop its characteristic Blue cheese flavor. The wheel has a locked-in flavor that cut, prewrapped pieces often lack.

5-lb. wheel $12.98 West of Rockies.
$13.98 East of Rockies.

Nichols Garden Nursery

Brick Cheese

"Cured" Brick cheese that is
between Brick and Limburger in
flavor. Not shipped during June,
July, and August.

Net wt. 5½ lb. $14.45

The Swiss Cheese Shop

Creamy Brick

An American original, Brick is so
mild, creamy, and satisfying that
people of all tastes enjoy its
old-fashioned flavor. Carefully
shelf-cured and aged to the peak of
smooth, mellow creaminess.

Net wt. 2 lb. $4.75

The Swiss Colony

Brie

Brie, the distinctly rich, semisoft
cheese from France with the full
delicious flavor. Brie is the most
elegant addition to appetizers or
desserts. Perfect with fine wines.

7 oz. $2.95

The Swiss Colony

French Brie Cheese

This one is sold by the kilogram; 1
kilogram (kg.) equals 2.20 pounds.

Golden Brie (extra rich, extra great):	1 kg.	$12.50
	2 kg.	$24.50
Normandy Brie (rich and creamy, yet mild):	1 kg.	$10.00
	2 kg.	$19.50

Caviarteria

Camembert

The "classic" dessert cheese, full of
ripe, rich flavor and aroma. The
choice of connoisseurs. Full-bodied
Camembert, from France, was
named by Napoleon and is the
epicurean choice for dessert the
world over.

7 oz. $2.95

The Swiss Colony

Aged Cheddar

A delightfully sharp and tangy wheel
of aged Cheddar. For the cheese
lover who appreciates the very best,
this is five pounds of perfect
pleasure.

Cheddar Pippin No. 18 $15.25

The Swiss Cheese Shop

Aged Sharp Cheddar

For those who enjoy old-fashioned
wheels of sharp Cheddar cheese,
Sugarbush has a limited number of
wheels that have been aged about two
years. This cheese is also available in
blocks, as shown below. This is
natural cheese aged the slow,
old-fashioned way.

6-lb. wheel $13.95. $2.35 postage
and handling
5½-lb. block $11.95. $2.35 postage
and handling
2-lb. block $6.50. $1.35 postage and
handling

Sugarbush Farms

Cheddar Bars

This is Vermont Cheddar, not colored, not processed, just natural cheese, country-cured with care. Sugarbush puts it up in foot-long bars that are perfect for cracker-size slices. Try either the natural country-aged Cheddar, or Henry VIII's favorite—Cheddar liberally sprinkled with sage—or the smoked bar, which is smoked golden for five days over a slow-burning maple-hickory log fire.

Sharp Cheddar Cheese bar $3.65
Foot-long Sage Cheese bar $3.65
Foot-long Hickory and Maple Cheese bar $3.65
Add $1.15 to the above prices for postage and handling

Sugarbush Farms

Sharp Cheddar Barrel

A delicious blending of the smoothest full-bodied creamy Cheddar cheeses and delicate seasonings. The black barrel contains 1¼ lb. of this special cheese.

$4.95

The Swiss Colony

Sharp Cheddar Barrel

A delicious, smooth-spreading blend, made from aged Cheddar. Packed in gold-foil barrels—serve right from the refrigerator. There's Sharp Cheddar, Cheddar with Port Wine, Cheddar with Bacon, and Cheddar with Pecans.

8 oz. $6.50 each

The Swiss Colony

Cheddar Blocks

This unusual cheese is fully and properly cured to bring it to peak perfection . . . to give it a delicious

smooth, zesty, mouth-watering flavor. It is aged for at least two years and held constantly at a uniform low temperature.

5-lb. block $14.95 (more in same parcel, $2.75 per lb.)
4-lb. block $11.85
3-lb. block $9.20
2-lb. block $6.65

John Harmon's Country Store

Cheddar Rolls

These large rolls add a touch of glamour to appetizer or dessert trays. Full-bodied, flavorful Cheddar is masterfully blended and rolled with the choicest nutmeats and flavorings. Rolls of Cheddar with Almonds, Paprika Cheddar with Port Wine, Cheddar with Walnuts, and Cheddar with Pecans.
2 7-oz. rolls and 2 10-oz. rolls $5.95

The Swiss Colony

Cheddar Spreads

Here are three delectable Cheddar spreads in handy, reusable pottery crocks. Six ounces each of Sharp Cheddar, Smoked Hickory Cheddar, and Bleu-Cheddar Blend. Some folks' buy this gift just to collect the crocks! But first, dispose of the cheese! It is special.

Order Gift No. 362 $9.95 delivered

Harry and David

Cheddar Wheel

A whole wheel of delicious sharp Cheddar cheese. Aged for 1½ years in temperature-controlled cellars.

3 lb. $9.50

Figi's

Raw Milk Sharp Cheddar

This cheese is for those who want the natural product. It is not colored or heat pasteurized to kill the beneficial milk bacteria or natural enzymes. Well aged, with that good Cheddar tang. Known as ''Rogue Gold,'' it is a speciality of southern Oregon.

2 lbs. $6.25 West of the Rockies.
$6.75 East of the Rockies.

Nichols Garden Nursery

Salt-Free Cheddar

This Cheddar is ideal for those on a salt-free diet. The same art of cheesemaking has gone into this cheese as in Nichols' other fine Cheddars. A specialty of Oregon.

1 lb. $3.95

Nichols Garden Nursery

Sharp Cheddar Kave Kure

A blend of natural aged cheeses. Tangy, smooth-spreading cheese handsomely packed in seal-tight earthenware crocks.

20 oz. $6.50
2½ lb. $9.95

Figi's

Smokehouse Cheddar

A whole wheel of Smokehouse Cheddar made from a special blend of rich Wisconsin Sharp Cheddars. The cheese is carefully smoked over natural embers to impart a slightly robust tang. Makes a ''pasteurized process cheese'' that is sensationally different.

2 lbs. $5.75

The Swiss Colony

Vermont Aged Cheddar

Most stores today sell skim-milk Cheddar that is about three months old. All Dakin Farm's cheese is between 12 and 30 months old and is made of whole Vermont milk.

2-lb. block 2-yr.-old Sharp $7.25, $7.65, $7.90
3-lb. wheel Best Cheddar 2-yr.-old Sharp $9.25, $9.50, $9.75
5-lb. wheel 2-yr.-old Sharp $14.50, $15.00, $15.50
(Prices vary according to delivery area.)

Dakin Farm

Vermont Cheddar Cheese

Made from whole natural milk with no added ingredients. It is aged nearly a year to a sharpness that makes it perfect for fondue, cheese sandwiches, or with crackers or apple pie.

5-lb. wheel $11.80 *or* $12.80
3-lb. wheel $7.55 *or* $8.20
(Prices vary according to delivery area.)

Green Mountain Sugar House

Shelf Aged To Perfection

Vermont CHEESE

Vermont Cheddar Cheese

Vermont Cheddar has been a cheese-lover's favorite for years. Mrs. Appleyard has added to her pantry all natural Cheddar cheese from the Cabot Farmers' Cooperative Creamery. Its traditional flavor is quality to enjoy.

3 8-oz. bars (Sharp, Mild, Sage) each individually wrapped and sealed $5.35, $5.60, $5.85
3-lb. wheel Mild Cheddar (aged 2–3 months) *or* 3-lb. wheel Sharp Cheddar (aged 8–10 months) $8.00, $8.25, $8.75
(Prices vary according to delivery area.)

The Appleyard Corporation

Vermont Cheddar Favorites

All the old Cheddar favorites—Sharp, Sage, Smoked, and Jack—all in identifying colored wax. Natural cheese self-aged to perfection.

3-lb. Cheddar wheel	$ 6.95
3-lb. Sage wheel	6.95
5-lb. Cheddar wheel	11.45
12-lb. Cheddar wheel	23.25
8-oz. Cheddar	2.15
1-lb. Cheddar	3.75
8-oz. Sage	2.15
8-oz. Smoked	2.15
1-lb. Smoked	3.75
1-lb. Trio	3.00
8-oz. Jack	2.15

Harwood Hill Orchard

Walnut-Cheddar Wheel

Choicest English walnuts and a smooth, buttery combination of rich Cheddar and creamy Swiss cheeses. To the light and creamy cheese is added a generous crusting of fine walnut pieces.

2 lb. 1½ oz. $7.95

The Swiss Colony

Wine Cheddar Barrels

Superb Cheddars, the cream of Wisconsin's dairies, take on a new flavor with the addition of Brandy, Port, and Sherry. Not a wine flavoring, but real wine, carefully mixed into the cheese.

3 4-oz. barrels $3.95

The Swiss Colony

Wine Cheddar Wheel

A delightfully rich combination of the creamiest Cheddar cheeses with mellow Port wine, carefully blended and sealed in a unique wax wheel. You can use this wheel as a dramatic centerpiece for a holiday table.

Net wt. 1½ lbs. $5.95

The Swiss Colony

Cheese in a Compote

Stainless-steel compote with Swiss Kave Kure Cheese Ball rolled in crunchy English walnuts. Compote measures 5 inches in diameter.

16-oz. ball $6.95

Figi's

Colby

This is a favorite of those who like a mild-flavored creamy-textured cheese.

Net wt. 2 lb. $5.95
Two or more shipments to same address $5.50 each

The Swiss Cheese Shop

Crowley's Colby Cheese

Appleyard's offers Crowley's Colby Cheese—Vermont's only handmade cheese. Soft and smooth-textured, Colby is sparingly salted and made only from raw milk delivered daily from neighboring farms to the old-fashioned cheese factory in Healdville. A Vermont tradition since 1824, Crowley's Colby is made by a time-honored process and has no additives, preservatives, or artificial substances.

3-lb. wheel Sharp (aged 8 months) *or* 3-lb. wheel Medium (aged 4–6 months) $8.75, $9.00, $9.50
5-lb. wheel Sharp *or* 5-lb. wheel Medium $12.00, $12.65, $13.50 (Prices vary according to delivery area.)

The Appleyard Corporation

Colby Wheel

Colby is a milder, moister form of Cheddar, with a "lacier" (more open) texture. The cheese of the Midwest, it is a delicious slicing cheese, perfect for cheese trays and informal parties. Beautifully waxed wheel.

2 lb. $5.50

The Swiss Colony

Goat Cheese

Made entirely from unpasteurized Grade A goat's milk by a skilled Wisconsin cheesemaker trained in Switzerland. There is a creamy white Brick aged 60 days; a tangy Caraway, a delicious blend of Brick spiced with caraway seeds and aged at least 60 days; a mellow Cheddar, a snow-white cheese with a rich Cheddar flavor, aged at least 60 days; and a zesty Swiss, believed to be the first Swiss cheese made out of goat's milk in the United States. It is manufactured in 200-pound wheels and carefully aged at least 120 days before cutting.

9 oz. Brick $2.25
9 oz. Caraway $2.25
7 oz. Cheddar $2.25
6 oz. Swiss $2.25

Diamond Diary Goat Farm

Jumbo Gouda

A great buttery wheel of Gouda—mild, wholesome, creamy butter flavor—is hard to improve. Red waxed ball, full of light, clean flavor.

2 lb. $5.95

The Swiss Colony

Green Mountain Bleu

A new Sugarbush cheese, rich and creamy, this is a hit with all Bleu cheese lovers. It makes a wonderful addition to salads as well as a fine spread for crackers. Because it is soft, it is put up in half-size bars only.

Half-size bar $3.65. Postage and handling $1.15

Sugarbush Farms

The Mail-Order Food Book

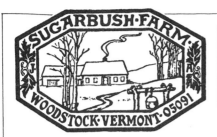

Green Mountain Jack

A delightfully mild cheese with a unique flavor that is hard to describe. It's an eastern variety of the famous Monterey Jack. Available in foot-long and half-size bars.

Foot-long bars $3.65.
Postage and handling $1.15

Sugarbush Farms

Switzerland Gruyère

Highly prized by the Swiss for its creamy color and rich, sweet flavor, Gruyère is made high up in the verdant Swiss Alpine meadows, cared for by time-honored methods, then carried to market.

1½ lb. $5.95

The Swiss Colony

Ham 'n' Cheese

A tasty combination of a one-pound imported Holland ham, boneless and ready-to-serve, and a delicious variety of cheeses: 2 oz. each of Wisconsin Colby, Brick, Edam, and Cheddar; three 1-oz. cheese links; and two 1-oz. pieces each of Kummel and Tilsit.

Ship wt. 3 lb. $8.50

Figi's

Hollander

Wooden-crated, plump wheels of choice Gouda, flavorful smoked Edam, and zesty Caraway-Gouda cheeses.

3 6-oz wheels $6.50

Figi's

Fresh Italian Cheeses

You will have to write the supplier for current prices on these cheeses.

Ricotta: fresh, white and fluffy as whipped cream cheese, Ricotta is the traditional filling for pastas. Also enjoyed in fresh, uncooked state with a sprinkling of salt or pepper, or as dessert with cinnamon. No mail orders.
Mozzarella: a cooking cheese for pizza or lasagna that comes in a 1-lb. ball. Also available smoked.
Mantecha: delicately seasoned and generously filled with a rich butter center. Comes in a small round ball, approximately 1½ lb.

Manganaro Foods

Mild Italian Table Cheeses

You will have to write the supplier for current prices on these cheeses.

Bel Paese: a world-famous mellow cheese from Italy. It is packed in 1-lb size and in 4-lb and 6-lb packages.
Fontina: a sweet, delicate flavor, similar to Swiss Gruyère in taste and texture.
Fonduta: a bland and gentle cheese similar to Muenster, popular for sandwiches and canapés.
Ricotta Romano: a creamy white mild cheese with a slightly salty flavor. Spreads easily on breadsticks and makes a pleasant complement to wine.
Taleggio: a mellow cheese with a slightly piquant flavor. It has a creamy soft, snow-white texture and makes a fine ending for a meal. Comes in 4-lb. to 6-lb. squares.
Feta: a semisoft, slightly salty table cheese from Greece.
Asiago: mild and smoky; an excellent after-dinner treat.

Manganaro Foods

Strong Italian Cheeses

These are hard-cheese favorites, for people with hearty cheese appetites. Write the supplier for current prices.

Cacciocavallo: has a sharp and robust flavor and is fine for grating; or slice it to serve with wine, bread, or fruit. Comes in 4-lb. to 6-lb. chunks shaped like pointed spindles.
Ragusano: a lighter version of Cacciocavallo, from the Ragusa district of Sicily, it is cured in long rectangular forms.
Incannestrata: distinguished by its braided-basket wrapping, this cheese is popular for its sharpness and bite.
Pepato: a bit sharper than Incannestrata from adding whole black peppercorns. Fine for grating or for table use. Comes in basket shape.
Pecorino di Tavola: sharp, semihard table cheese. Comes in wheels of 4 lb. to 6 lb.

Manganaro Foods

Kreme Kaese (Cream Havarti)

A creamy mild cheese, rich in color and flavor with small "eyes" and a semifirm texture. Perfect for cheese trays and sandwiches and a piquant addition to fruits.

2 lb. $6.95

The Swiss Colony

Liederkranz

A magnificent dessert favorite available only from Van Wert, Ohio, this ripe, milder form of Limburger is a natural for all who love full-bodied, soft-ripened, flavorful dessert cheeses.

2 ¼-lb. cheeses $2.95

The Swiss Colony

Limburger

This Alpine Brand Limburger needs no description. It is super. Comes cleaned and ready for the table. This cheese is not shipped during June, July, and August.

Net wt. 30 oz. $5.95
Three or more 15 oz. shipped to same address $2.60 each

The Swiss Cheese Shop

Muenster

A "German type" mild cheese that is excellent for sandwiches.

Net wt. 2 lb. $5.95
Two or more shipped to same address $5.50 each

The Swiss Cheese Shop

Wisconsin Muenster

Semisoft, very mild, with an irresistible, subtle "butteriness" that calls you back for more. Similar to fine Brick cheese, but a lighter, more delicate flavor.

2 lb. $5.40

The Swiss Colony

Parmesan

This flavorful cheese is creamy white, very hard and granular, and mild in flavor. It is sold in pieces, wedges, and grated. Use it in grated form on lasagna, spaghetti, and pizza; or sprinkle over soups and salads. Write the supplier to obtain a price list.

Purity Cheese Company

Creamy Port Salut

Trappist monks at Port du Salut in France originated this cheese from a secret formula. It has a subtle, full-bodied flavor—mild, but richly so—and a semisoft, creamy texture.

2½ lb. $6.95

The Swiss Colony

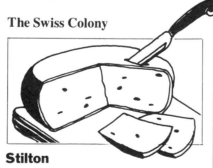

Stilton

Stilton has been called the "king of cheeses." Take a five-pound piece of aged English Stilton, a silver cheese scoop, and some English biscuits. Then add Port wine—and purr!

5-lb. piece $38.75

Maison Glass

Center-cut Swiss Cheese

Cut out of the "heart" of Wisconsin's finest full-cream Swiss, this cheese is fully aged and selected for its fine flavor and texture.

Net wt. 2 lb. $6.95
Two or more shipped to same address $6.50 each

The Swiss Cheese Shop

Smoked Swiss Cheese

This is very old and tangy Swiss cheese that has been smoked over hickory fires for 48 hours. The unique flavor is recommended for gourmets only.

Net wt. 30 oz. $7.25
Two or more shipped to same address $6.80 each

The Swiss Cheese Shop

Swiss Cheese Wheel

This butter-rich Swiss cheese wheel is a replica of the 175-lb. wheels of golden, nut-sweet Swiss Cheese. Mild and buttery.

5-lb. wheel $13.95

The Swiss Colony

Swiss Cheese Wheels

Miniature wheels of Swiss cheese that have been aged to bring out their full nutlike flavor. This cheese makes an ideal gift for someone, including you.

Net wt. 4½ lb. (1 wheel) $13.95
Two or more wheels shipped to same address $12.80 each

The Swiss Cheese Shop

The Mail-Order Food Book

PASTA

Deboles Pasta

	24 8-oz. boxes
Fettucini (wide)	$14.40
Linguine (medium)	14.40
Macaroni Shells	14.40
Spaghetti	14.40
Spinach Linguine	14.40
Spinach Spaghetti	14.40
Ziti	14.40

Infinity Foods

"Paprikas" Homemade Pasta

In a never-ending variety of twists and twirls, each is made of the finest semolina, the golden, sugar-free flour from the heart of Durum wheat, and the yolks of country-fresh eggs. Shapes and sizes include: Egg Barley—Tarhonya, Large Egg Noodle Squares—Kockateszta, Small Egg Noodle Squares (for soup), Shell Noodles—Cavatelli, German-style Spaetzle, Italian-style Macaroni, Extra Fine Soup Noodles, Medium Noodles, Broad Noodles, Large Bowties, Small Bowties. Order a selection.

1 lb. $1.59
5 lb. $7.50
10 lb. $14.00

Paprikas Weiss

Le Jardin Polenta

A popular Italian delicacy.

16 oz. $.95

Le Jardin du Gourmet

Maggi Spaetzle

A fine-quality egg noodle product that is ready to serve in minutes. It's excellent with goulash and a fitting accompaniment to wild game or other meat specialities.

10½-oz box $2.98
5 boxes $13.00
10 boxes $24.00

Paprikas Weiss

Wholewheat Spaghetti

Made from stoneground 100 percent whole grain Durum whole wheat flour.

Price obtainable on request from supplier.

Chico-San

Variety of Farinaceous Foods

A potpourri of world favorites

Falafel Mix 16-oz. box 2.50
Gnocchi 16-oz. bag 1.75
Polenta 16-oz. box 1.75

Maison Glass

Wild Rice is not really a rice—but it is really wild. A grain unlike all others, high in vitamins and protein, no one has been able to cultivate it successfully.

Canadian/Minnesotan Wild Rice

This is wild rice of the finest grade hand picked, carefully parched, and painstakingly sorted to include only the longest, tenderest kernels. The best wild rice is hard and needs to cook for a long time, but its incredible flavor makes the extra effort seem trivial. One pound will serve 15 to 20 hungry people as a perfect accompaniment to wild game, fish, or fowl. Wild rice makes an exciting gift to anyone interested in the art of cooking.

¼-lb. pkg. $1.75
1-lb. pkg. $6.00
5 lbs. or more $5.00 per lb.

Northwestern Coffee Mills

Mahnomen Wild Rice

Wild Rice was called *Mahnomen* by the Indians, meaning "good berry." This was a perfect description, for in addition to its unique flavor and quality, wild rice is also more nutritious than ordinary rice. No wild game dinner is complete without wild rice; yet it is also delicious with just melted butter and salt.
The Sioux and Algonquin prized wild rice, and fought repeated battles for the wild-rice territory in Minnesota and Wisconsin. They fought wars; you can get it simply by ordering it from Gokeys.

1-lb. bag $6.50

Gokey's

Minnehaha Wild Rice

Minnehaha, a legendary member of the great Sioux nation, has been linked for years with the proud and romantic history of the Sioux. This product is named for her because her forebears found it and handed it down. The Indians often mixed wild rice with other grains, especially maize. That's still a good idea. The distinctive flavor of the wild grain is such that fowl and game hunters crave it. All gourmets seek it when they want to add a special touch to the most sophisticated cuisine.

5-lb. box $29.50
1-lb. box $6.85

Minnehaha Wild Rice Co.

At the present time we are unable to quote any coffee prices. All the coffees listed here are delicious and worth trying, but please contact the supplier for his current price list before ordering.

Coffee Blends

Coffee blends are formulated to suit widely varied tastes. To create a blend, two or more coffees are mixed to gain a different and desirable taste, without primary regard to the cost of the ingredients. The goal is to find a combination of coffee aroma, body, and flavor that is more satisfying than any of the individual coffees comprising the blend. The full body, pleasant aroma, and exciting taste of the blends show the customer why the company uses only the very best beans.

Hawaiian Kona Blend—nurtured by the volcanic soil on the slopes of Mauna Loa, Kona coffee has a superior and distinctive mild flavor.

It is balanced with the aroma of rich Central American coffees.

Mocha Java Blend—perhaps the most famous coffee blend because of the near-perfect match of Java's creamy richness and Mocha's piquant taste. The blend of these exotic coffees creates the ultimate in coffee.

New Orleans Chicory Blend—a time-honored combination of South American coffee and roasted chicory root. The chicory lends a pleasant

taste that evokes visions of antebellum New Orleans. Available ground only.

Northwestern Coffee Mills

Coffee Blends

Dennis Blend—a combination of fancy East African Arabica coffees with high-grown Central American and Colombian beans gives a tantalizing flavor that is rich and winey.

Ryan Blend—specially selected high-grown Central American coffees combine to give fine flavor and aroma, and a rich, full-bodied taste that will delight the most discriminating coffee lover.

Tanzania Peaberry—a fancy Arabica coffee with a winey taste that is light and flavorful.

Simpson and Vail

Coffee Straights

These straights are coffees of special merit, each in its own right. Some are readily available, some are scarce, and some are rare, much as with vintage wines. All the straights are freshly roasted before sale, and are packaged without the taste-altering addition of other coffees. The straights can provide the excitement of discovering the widely different taste sensations of coffees grown in different areas of the world. They can also be used to create new blends in search of the perfect cup of coffee.

Celebes Kalossi—one of the rarest of Northwestern coffees. It has the refined flavor of other East Indian coffees but is balanced between

NORTHWESTERN COFFEE MILLS
217 N. Broadway • Milwaukee, Wis. 53202

Java's robust body and Sumatra's clean taste.

Mexican Altura—sometimes called Coatepec, this coffee has a delightful, fresh taste with a delicate aroma. It is fairly mild, with a hint of nutty flavor. Recommended as the straight for those who prefer a light coffee.

Northwestern Coffee Mills

Coffee Straights

Djimmah—a rare coffee from Ethiopia that is flavorful but light; spicy bouquet.

Guatemalan—for those who search for a lighter, more subtle cup, this tangy flavor is perfect.

Java—a most desirable, sturdy flavor; a truly distinctive body.

Maracaibo—the pride of Venezuela, roasted with a high regard for the aromatic and winey quality of the beans.

Schapira Coffee Company

Decaffeinated Coffee

For those who find caffeine a trial, this decaffeinated 100% Colombian is similar in taste to a mild Central American coffee. Most other decaffeinated coffees are processed from lower-grade coffee beans, with poor-tasting results. This decaffeinated can be purchased in the whole-bean form to be freshly ground.

Northwestern Coffee Mills

French Market Coffee

This is New Orleans' famous coffee—a blend of coffee and chicory that makes a delicious cup of coffee. Available in one-pound tins.

Kate Latter's

Green Coffee Straights

Green, or raw, coffee straights are available to those who wish to experiment with roasting their own coffee. Northwestern offers their straight coffees at $.50 per pound less than their list price for the same roasted coffee.

Northwestern Coffee Mills

Green Coffees

African
Aged Mocha
Bolivian
Brazilian Peaberry
Brazilian Santos
Colombian Medellin
Costa Rican
Mexican

Empire Coffee and Tea Company

Individual Instant Coffee Packets

Brand Name	Amount
Calma (decaffeinated)	35 pks.
Sanka (decaffeinated)	100 pks.
Sanka (freeze-dried decaffeinated)	80 pks.
Taster's Choice (regular freeze-dried)	100 pks.
Taster's Choice (freeze-dried decaffeinated)	100 pks.

Empire Coffee and Tea Company

Instant Coffee

Brand	Jar Size
Caffe Vivo (espresso)	2 oz.
Cappuccino	1¾ oz.
French Market (with chicory)	4 oz.
Irish style	2 oz.
Jamaican Blue Mountain (regular)	2-oz.
Lord Calvet (regular)	6 oz.
Mocha (decaffeinated)	1¾ oz.

Empire Coffee and Tea Company

Dark Roast Coffees

American Roasts
    Altura Coatepec: mellow, nutlike
      Mexican
    Java: the genuine; rich and nutty
      Maracaibo: mild, low-acid
      Venezuelan
    Santos Bourbon: extremely mild
      Brazilian
French Roasts
    Altura Coatpec: rich, dark
      Mexican
    Colombian: sharp, robust.
      Continental style

McNulty's Tea and Coffee Co.

Dark Roast Coffees

An important variable in the taste of coffee is the length of time used in roasting the raw coffee beans. Most dark coffees are a rich brown American roast, neither light and tasteless nor burned and bitter. Dark roasts are created by keeping the coffee in the oven longer than for regular American roasts, with the flames set lower to roast evenly without burning. The resulting rich, extra-roasted taste and glossy, dark beans distinguish these dark roast coffees.

Espresso Roast—also known as Italian roast. The espresso roasted bean is black-brown and glistens with coffee oil. As with French roast, espresso has great potential in recipes as well as by itself. Warm milk, hot chocolate, or a twist of lemon are recommended company for espresso's penetrating robust flavor.

French Roast—also known as Continental roast. A deep brown roast with the coffee's oil brought to the surface of the bean. This roast is the favorite of many Central and South American coffee drinkers as well as European consumers. Although only slightly darker than American roast, French roast has a heartier body and sharper taste.

Northwestern Coffee Mills

Black Tea

Black tea is fully fermented tea. First the leaves are rolled, which accelerates a natural fermentation process by releasing oxidizing enzymes. The fermentation is stopped by heating the leaves at high temperature. The best tea is heated, or fired, as it is termed in the tea trade, at precisely the right moment, with the leaves being under- or overfermented. The type of firing process is sometimes used to describe the tea, such as "baked fired" tea or "pan fired" tea.

Assam Tea—the strongest tea, pungent and brisk in flavor. Grown in the Assam district of eastern India, this tea has a mellow body that makes it outstanding in its own right or when its distinctive character is added to any blend.   ¼ lb. $1.45

Darjeeling, second flush—grown in the foothills of the Indian Himalayas. Darjeeling has a reddish color and a very fragrant aroma. Its exciting bouquet is unique among teas. The finest grade of Darjeeling is the rarest and costliest of the black teas, the second flush, or picking, of the best tea bushes.   1/4 lb. $1.65

Northwestern Coffee Mills

Eastern Teas

Fabulous flavors of India and the Orient are combined in these nine beautifully boxed tins: ¾-oz. Ceylon Breakfast, Rare Mandarin, Lapsang Souchong, Jasmine, and India & Ch'a Ching; ⅞-oz. Mint and English Breakfast; and ⅝-oz. Formosa Oolong.

Assortment above $5.95

The Swiss Colony

F & M Tea Jar

Mason's ironstone jar, F & M clock design, comes with ½ pound of Royal Blend Tea—a traditional English tea.

Approx. $16.00

Fortnum & Mason

Grace Teas

By importing directly from growers in the Orient, Grace Tea can procure teas that are reasonable in price, freshly packed, and at the peak of their flavor. These teas surpass commercial grades of tea by far, and are even considerably better than teas packed in England for the U.S. market.

Superb Darjeeling 6000—extra high quality. This superb tea, especially picked from the early summer flush, has an unsurpassed flavor and aroma. ½ lb. $4.90

Winey Keenun—especially fine English breakfast tea easily recognized by its fine silvery leaf. Has a smooth winey flavor of real distinction.
½ lb. $4.00

Lapsang Souchong Smokey No. 1 —a unique tea of great aroma made by the hand-fired method, and the best of the rare Lapsong smoky teas.
½ lb. $4.00

Grace Tea Co.

Green Tea

Green tea is not allowed to ferment. The leaves are fired immediately after picking. Some green teas are picked as young buds rather than leaves, and some are rolled differently—the gunpowder green is an example. Green teas are the lowest in caffeine content of all teas.

Gunpowder Green Tea—peahead gunpowder green, which means that it has the fresh taste of young tea buds. It has been rolled into tight balls instead of the usual twisted leaves, giving it its name, in that it looks similar to buckshot. It has the most flowery taste of the green teas, and has the pronounced sharp green-tea body.   ¼ lb. $1.40

Panfired Formosa Green—light in the cup with a mellow, tart taste that sweetens well with honey.
¼ lb. $1.45

Northwestern Coffee Mills

Herb Teas

Mo's 24 Herb Tea—an unusual combination of hibiscus, peppermint, spearmint, raspberry leaves, eucalyptus, chamomile, red clover tops, anise seed, rosehips, strawberry leaves, comfrey, alfalfa, rosemary, papaya, blackberry, mullein, nettles, goldenrod, elder flowers, catnip, plantain, sage and yarrow. Flavor is mountain fresh and woodsy.
½ lb. $2.00

Red Zinger—contains rosehips, hibiscus flowers, lemon grass, orange peel, peppermint, and wild cherry bark. The fruit of the rose gives Red Zinger a citrus fruit taste and a wholesome feeling. Lemon grass, a delicious Mexican herb, combined with orange peel and wild cherry bark, gives Red Zinger its spirit. Peppermint, the world's most powerful single herb, completes Red Zinger with a bolt of powerful freshness. It cheers tired taste buds, is an exciting flavor iced or hot, and may be combined with fruit juices to create an unusual soft-drink experience. Recommended to people trying herb teas for the first time.
½ lb. $1.95

Celestial Seasonings

Erewhon's Herb Teas

Big Saikoto	$.95
Boi-Oghito	.58
Cay Lily Tea	.88
Jewel's Tea	.73
Nine Taste Tea	.73
Two Peony Tea	.44

(Order the above in multiples of 5 units. Each unit consists of 12 bags.)

Bancha (Japanese green tea)

12 4-oz.	$13.20
1 lb.	$3.75

Erewhon

Fmali Herb Teas

	24 bags	1 lb.
Lemon Mist	$.65	$2.15
Matte Mint	.60	1.50
Pelican Punch	.58	2.50
Sleepytime	.75	3.25

The Fmali Company

Gourmet Specialty Teas

Cinnamon	1 oz.	$ .35		
Gourmet Anisette	1 oz.	1.00		
Orange Mint Spice	½ lb.	3.00	1 lb.	$6.00
Orange Spice	½ lb.	2.50	1 lb.	5.00

McNulty's Tea and Coffee Co.

Herb Tea Bags

Bags of herb tea come in many flavors: peppermint, chamomile, sassafras root, sassafras leaves, rosehips with hibiscus, alfalfa mint, and papaya mint.

48 bags $1.75

McNulty's Tea and Coffee Co.

CELESTIAL SEASONINGS®

MAKERS OF FINE HERB TEAS FOR THE WHOLE FAMILY

RED ZINGER® herb tea   SLEEPYTIME herb tea   MATTÉ ORANGE SPICE herb tea

Loose Teas

	Per lb.
Assam	$3.25
Assam/Darjeeling Mixture	3.75
Ceylon-Small leaf	2.70
China Black	5.98
Earl Grey	4.25
English Breakfast	3.00
Fancy Indian	2.70
Indonesian	2.60
Irish Style Black	3.15
Java Superior	4.25
Mint Tea	5.00
Russian Black	3.00
Turkish Black	4.00

Empire Coffee and Tea Company

McNulty's Teas

These are imported from the best tea gardens of the Orient and are packed straight or custom blended on the premises. Check with supplier for current prices.

Black teas include First Harvest Darjeeling; Choice Assam, and Irish Assam; Ceylon teas and Chinese teas.

Green teas are the Japanese teas including Uji-Gyokura and Uji-No Sato.

Oolong teas are Tikuanyin, Ming Xiang, China, and Formosa Oolong.

Gourmet specialty teas:

Orange Spice	1 lb.	$5.00
Orange Mint Spice	1 lb.	6.00
Lavender Tea	1 oz.	1.00
Jamaican Ginger Tea	1 oz.	.70

Tea bags (48 bags per box):

Assam	$1.50
Darjeeling	2.00
English Breakfast	1.50
Formosa Oolong	1.25

McNulty's Tea and Coffee Co.

Mixed Teas

The following can be obtained: Alfalfa, Borage, Cascara Bark, Comfrey Leaf, Cramp Bark, Dandelion Root, Elderflowers, Eucalyptus Leaves, Fenugreek Seed, Lime Flowers.

Any 6 $5.00

Nichols Garden Nursery

Mixed Teas

Colonial Tea—peppermint, cloves, nutmeg, and citrus peel. A favorite of the early colonists who settled in the Rocky Hollow Valley. 1 oz. $1.05

Kittatinny Tea—lemon verbena, rosebuds, chamomile, and rosemary. A lovely lemon fragrance that is cooling on a warm summer evening and a gracious afternoon tea.
½ oz. $.85

Rocky Hollow Herb Farm

Mormon or Squaw Tea

Tea foliage is taken from a small shrub resembling a miniature pine tree, which grows in the high deserts of Nevada, Utah, and California. The pine needlelike foliage is gathered at elevations of 5000 to 8000 feet, where nature is pure and clean, untainted by chemical pollutants.

4 lb. $16.95

Nichols Garden Nursery

Oolong Teas

Oolong Tea—leaves are dried, rolled and fired quickly, which produces a semi-fermented tea with a taste halfway between that of a green and that of a black tea. Aroma is generally described as fruity.
¼ lb. $1.45

Formosa Oolong—oolong rich and fruity in the cup. It has been painstakingly harvested and processed, yielding a subtle, fine taste and evenly colored leaves. It is graded "finest" by the Taiwan government.
¼ lb. $1.45

Northwestern Coffee Mills

Scented Teas

Jasmine—all the promise and mystery of the Orient in the fine taste of this delicious tea containing jasmine flower petals 1 lb. $3.50

Lapsang Smoky Souchong—a distinctive smoky flavor unlike any other tea 1 lb. $3.50

Mint-in-Tea—an excellent example of that famous southern-style tea. Cool and refreshing, it is also superb when iced. 1 lb. $3.50

Simpson and Vail

Jasmine and Orange Scented Teas

Jasmine Blossom Blend—a scented oolong tea. Most of the oolongs come from mainland China. Whole jasmine blossoms give a distinct, sharp, flowery flavor to this exotic tea.
¼ lb. $1.50

Orange Spiced Blend—the romance of the scent of cloves and orange with the very best of black teas. It is considered to have a fresher taste than the fine "Constant Comment" tea. It makes an excellent iced tea.
¼ lb. $1.50

Northwestern Coffee Mills

Schapira Teas

Best Ceylon—all the qualities of an excellent all-purpose tea. The flavor is clear and strong. 1 lb. $2.45

China Green—light, slightly tart flavor, pale green color, haunting fragrance.
1 lb. $3.50

Earl Grey—a truly exotic beverage. Teas from China and India are scented in the English manner. An afternoon tea.   1 lb. $3.75

Schapira Coffee Company

Taste Test Assortment

Caravel invites you to choose your favorite tea and be assured of the utmost in everyday flavor enjoyment by having your orders "custom blended" and packed to your own requirements. This is an adventure in flavor.

16 tins of all Caravel teas $3.95
Individual tins $.35 each
Caravel Coffee Company

Vintage Teas

Clapp has gathered together six of the world's rarest and most precious teas. They come packaged in attractive miniature wooden tea chests and weigh from 4 to 6 ounces each, depending on the type of tea. They are also available in a sampler containing 2 ounces each of the six teas.

China Keemun—the "Burgundy" of teas, heady, full-bodied

China Jasmine—golden green tea gently touched with the innocence of jasmine blossoms

China Oolong—a keen and tangy tea tamed by the delicate flavor of peach blossoms

China Yunnan—a wickedly exciting tea that is a rare jewel among Far Eastern teas

Darjeeling—the aromatic tea of India with the subtle flavor of black currant

Formosa Oolong—carefully semi-fermented to offer the briskness of black tea without sacrificing the tenderness of green tea

Individual chest	$7.50
Sampler	$5.00

O. H. Clapp & Co.

Twining's Teas

Twining's is the oldest firm of tea merchants in England. The present seventh generation of the family zealously guards the reputation by maintaining invariably high quality in every blend. Individual teas come in tins.

	½ lb.	1 lb.
Ceylon Breakfast Tea—a blend of full-flavored Ceylon, smooth-drinking, extremely palatable	$3.60	$6.95
Darjeeling Tea—a choice blend of Darjeeling fragrant black teas, light bodied, delicate, and mellow	3.60	6.95
Earl Grey's Tea—a world-famous blend of rare fancy teas of exceptional fragrance	3.60	6.95
Irish Breakfast Tea—traditional Irish blend of Assam and Ceylon teas, producing a pungent, dark, amber brew	3.25	
Queen Mary's Tea—a superb hill-grown Darjeeling tea with a Muscatel bouquet, supplied to Queen Mary	4.35	8.50

	per box
Twining Tea Sampler #1—a red Gift Box containing ¼-lb. tin each of Earl Grey's Tea, Queen Mary's Tea, Lapsang Souchong Tea, and English Breakfast Tea	$10.50
Twining Tea Sampler #2—a white Gift Box containing ¼-lb. tin each of Prince of Wales Tea, Formosa Oolong, Darjeeling, and Ceylon Breakfast Tea	10.25

Maison Glass

CONDIMENTS

Appleyard's Sampler

A delicious introduction to products from the Appleyard is a sample box containing your choice of two jars of either chutney, conserve, or apple cider jelly. They contain no additives or artificial preservatives. Once you try these savory products you'll want to keep an extra on hand for special occasions or as a welcome gift.

Apple Cider Jelly—a traditional Vermont favorite. Only pure cider from the Green Mountain State's best apples goes into making this sweet yet tangy jelly. Irresistible on hot muffins or toast.

Tomato Chutney—a spicy condiment that is perfect with curry, meat, seafood, or as an hors d'oeuvre. Blended together over a three-day period are fresh citrus fruits, tomatoes, spices, and maple syrup.

Tomato Conserve—simmered together for three days in small batches, conserve is a combination of

fresh oranges, lemons, raisins, apples, cinnamon, and maple syrup. This is a pleasing addition to the relish tray.
Any 2 9-oz. jars $3.65, $3.90, $4.25, depending on delivery area.

The Appleyard Corporation

Creole Treats by Trappey's

Here are two gift assortments that are sure to delight the gourmet.

Gift Box No. 1: includes Green Devil Peppers, Chef-Magic Kitchen Seasonings, Spice-up Table Seasonings, Remoulade Sauce, Mex-Pep Hot Sauce, Steak and Fish Sauce, Barbeque Sauce, Worcestershire Sauce, Indi-Pep Pepper Sauce. $12.95

Gift Box No. 2: includes Green Tabasco Peppers, Chef-Magic Kitchen Seasonings, Spice-up Table Seasoning, Remoulade Sauce, Trappey's Pepper Sauce, Worcestershire Sauce, Hot Pickled Okra, Mild Pickled Okra, Torrida Peppers, Dulcito Peppers. $14.95

Kate Latter's

Major Grey's Chutney

Bottled in Bombay, Sun brand's authentic East Indian chutney is prepared from the choicest mangoes, raisins, spices, and seasonings. Comes in a jar.

8½ oz. $1.60
17 oz. $3.00

Le Jardin du Gourmet

Mustard

Brand	Size	Price
Coleman's Hot Mustard	6-oz. jar	$1.25
Dijon Mustard, Gentilly, France	5½-oz. crock	1.95
Dijon Mustard (Tarragon) (Maille)	7-oz. jar	1.25
Maitre Jacque, salt-free	7½-oz. jar	1.25
Moutarde au poivre from Madagasgar	9-oz. crock	2.75
Savora	6¾-oz. jar	1.75

Maison Glass

Sweet 'n' Sour Salad Dressing

A delightful blend of maple sugar and maple vinegar make this a unique and delicious dressing for salads or barbeques.

1 lb. $1.10

Harwood Hill Orchard

Remoulade Sauce

This is a world-famous sauce. Its spicy, piquant flavor adds zest to seafood cocktails or salads.

3 10-oz. jars $9.50

Creole Delicacies

Sauce Salade

Sauce Salade is an ideal dressing for tomatoes, fresh from your garden! It is delicious with raw and cooked vegetables—artichokes, broccoli, cucumbers, cauliflower—and also excellent with fried fish and pork.

10½-oz. bottle $1.95

Maison Glass

Nichols Country Pork Sausage Seasoning

This seasoning comes from an old New England recipe using 12 different spices and herbs. It enables you to make delicious country pork sausage with that old-time flavor right in your own kitchen. Just use it with the ground pork from your butcher. Four ounces makes six pounds of sausage.

4 oz. $1.60

Nichols Garden Nursery

San Francisco Seasoning

A special blend of freeze-dried herbs and spices gives this a really great taste. Delicious on meats, fish, poultry, as dressings for salad, or as a topping for vegetables. Comes in an apothecary jar.

1¼ oz. $2.50
4 oz. $5.00

Calico Kitchen

Sauces and Dressings

Anchovy sauce (England)	3¾-oz. bottle	$1.00
Bearnaise sauce mix (Switzerland)	to make 1½ cups	.50
Harvey's sauce (England)	6-oz. bottle	.75
Hollandaise sauce	6½-oz. jar	1.50
Horseradish dressing	5-oz. jar	1.50
Raisin sauce	8-oz. jar	1.50
Sherry peppers (hot, concentrated)	5-oz. bottle	4.50
Newburg sauce	13-oz. tin	1.35
Basil sauce (pesto)	3¼-oz. jar	1.25

Maison Glass

Sherry Wine Vinegar

Made in Jerez de la Frontera, Spain, this vinegar is produced by the same natural *solera* system used to make the world's finest sherries. Each bottle of vinegar is at least 8 years old, and some of the wines used to make it are over 30. As this is a vintage product, the vinegar is quite strong and should be used sparingly. This vinegar does not need to be refrigerated and improves with time after it is opened.

1½ pt. $5.00

Maison Glass

HERBS, SPICES, SEASONINGS, AND FLAVORINGS

The prices quoted in the following section are from Aphrodisia, 28 Carmine Street, New York, N.Y. 10014.

Other companies carrying the full spectrum of herbs and spices are:

Casa Moneo
Erewhon
The Fmali Company
Harvest Health Herbs
The Herb Lady
Indiana Botanic Gardens
Infinity Foods

Lekvar By The Barrel
Le Jardin du Gourmet
Magic Garden Herb Co.
Maison Glass
Manganaro Foods
Nature's Herb Company
Nichol's Garden Nursery
Northwestern Coffee Mills
Rocky Hollow Herb Farm
Wide World of Herbs

Absinthe

According to legend, this plant, also known as *wormwood,* was driven out of the Garden of Eden. Commercially, absinthe is used to flavor Vermouth and is part of many homemade "bitters."

¼ lb. $2.15
1 lb. $7.50

Agar Agar

This is a gelatinous substance derived from seaweed. It is used as a vegetable substitute for animal gelatin or in jams, jellies, and soups. In cooking, use approximately one tablespoon to each cup of boiling water.

¼ lb. $4.55
1 lb. $17.00

Agrimony

Also known as *church steeples, sticklewort,* and *cocklebur,* this is an astringent herb much used in folk-remedies. Brewed as a tea flavored with licorice, agrimony was often taken as a spring tonic. As a natural dye, agrimony will turn fabric yellow.

¼ lb. $1.75
1 lb. $5.50

Alfalfa Leaf

As a source of vitamin K and iron, this is often brewed into a tasty tea. Use alfalfa alone or blended with other herbs. Add the leaves to such foods as soups, salads, and cooked vegetables.

¼ lb. $1.35
1 lb. $4.50

Allspice

The dried, unripe berry of a tree native to the Western Hemisphere, allspice was discovered by Christopher Columbus. He carried it back to Europe where it was called ''all'' spice because its aroma suggests a blend of cinnamon, cloves, and nutmeg. Use it whole in soups, gravies, pickling liquids, and spiced drinks. Grind it for use in fruitcakes, relishes, preserves, pies.

¼ lb. $2.15
1 lb. $7.50

Angelica Root

Also called *masterwort* or *archangel,* this was believed to bloom on the feast day of Michael the Archangel (May 8). Used in many popular perfumes and liqueurs.

¼ lb. $1.75
1 lb. $6.15

Anise Seed

A native of Asia Minor, anise is probably the oldest known aromatic seed. Anise has a licoricelike taste and is often used to flavor sweet pickles, vegetable and fruit salads, cakes, cookies, candies, stews, liqueurs.

¼ lb. $1.95
1 lb. $6.85

Arrowroot

The powdered root of a plant, arrowroot is indigenous to tropical America. The name *arrowroot* comes from the mistaken belief that it was an antidote for the poisoned arrows of the Indians of the West Indies. Arrowroot is an excellent thickening agent and is often used in place of cornstarch or flour.

¼ lb. $.50
1 lb. $1.85

Basil

Also known as *sweet basil,* this fragrant herb is native to India and Persia but now grows all over the world. It has often been called the ''herb of kings'' and is a symbol of love. Basil adds a warm flavor to foods and is especially good in thick, brown meat soups; classic tomato and turtle soups; or pizza and spaghetti sauces.

¼ lb. $1.55
1 lb. $5.50

Bayberry Bark

Also called *candleberry, waxberry, and wax myrtle,* this bitter bark is used as an ingredient in gargles, tonics, or incense. It can also be brewed into a tea.

¼ lb. $2.85
1 lb. $10.00

Bay Leaves

The ancient Greeks used *laurel leaves* (as bay leaves are also known) for making crowns for Olympic heroes and poets. Now used mainly as a cooking condiment in soups and chowders, pot roasts, etc., bay leaves add a strong, pungent, spicy touch to potpourris and sachets.

¼ lb. $1.25
1 lb. $4.50

Calamus Root

Sweet flag or *sweet sedge,* as it is also commonly known, has a pleasant taste and aroma. It can be candied and eaten in the same way as angelica. In perfumery, calamus is used as a fixative and adds a mellow spicy note to potpourris.

¼ lb. $1.95
1 lb. $6.85

Caraway Seeds

These crescent-shaped seeds are reputed to strengthen the memory and cure fickleness in lovers. Best known for use in rye bread, they are also good with spreads and dips, roasts, marinades, and salads (especially cole slaw).

¼ lb. $1.55
1 lb. $5.50

Cardamom

Native to India, these aromatic seeds were brought to Scandinavia by the Vikings and became a necessary ingredient in cooking. Also used in Swedish meatballs, Danish pastries, pies, marinades, and many curries.

Whole white	1 oz.	$1.50
	¼ lb.	5.25
Whole green	1 oz.	.90
	¼ lb.	3.20
Whole black	1 oz.	1.30
	¼ lb.	3.70
Ground	1 oz.	1.10
	¼ lb.	3.20

Cayenne Pepper

Also called *African pepper,* this very hot red pepper is named after the Cayenne region of South America where it was originally grown; now it comes mainly from Asia. It should be used sparingly and is good in a variety of dishes.

¼ lb. $1.35
1 lb. $3.95

The Mail-Order Food Book

Established 1970

MGHC

Chili Peppers, Very Hot

These peppers lend flavor and "bite" to soups, stews, gravies, pickles, relishes, and the like. Chilies are important in Indian, Middle Eastern, and Mexican cookery.

¼ lb. $1.35
1 lb. $4.70

Chili Powder

This is a blend of ground chili peppers and other herbs and spices. Use it in chili con carne, cheese sauces, dips.

¼ lb. $1.55
1 lb. $5.50

Chives, French

The mildest of the onion family, French chives may be used generously in salads, cheese dishes, omelets, and soups.

¼ lb. $3.70
1 lb. $13.00

Cinnamon

This well-known spice is actually the dried inner bark of a fragrant Asian tree. Ground, it may be used in pies, cakes, spiced beverages, meat and poultry dishes. Sticks make great swizzle sticks in punches, hot tea, chocolate drinks, mulled wine.

Ground: ¼ lb. $1.35
1 lb. $4.70
Sticks: ¼ lb. $1.95
1 lb. $6.85

Cloves

From the French *clou* ("nail"), this spice is the unopened bud of an evergreen tree indigenous to the Moluccas (Spice Islands). Cloves are used in spiced drinks, pickled fruits

Celery Flakes

These are the leaves and flaked stalks of celery that have been dehydrated. They are used in soups, stews, sauces, stuffings.

¼ lb. $1.55
1 lb. $5.50

Celery Seed

Available whole or ground, this is an excellent condiment with fish, soups, tomato juice, potato salad, eggs, cheese spreads.

¼ lb. $1.15
1 lb. $4.00

Celery Salt

This is ground celery seed mixed with salt; it is used in much the same way as salt.

¼ lb. $.75
1 lb. $2.75

Chamomile

The Spanish call this fragrant herb *manzanilla* ("little apple") and use it to flavor one of their best sherries. It is one of the most popular herb teas, with a sweet applelike aroma.

¼ lb. $1.55
1 lb. $5.50

and vegetables, marinades, cakes and cookies. Cloves are pungent ingredients in potpourris and sachets.

Whole: ¼ lb. $2.35
1 lb. $8.25
Ground: ¼ lb. $2.35
1 lb. $8.25

Candied Coriander

Eaten as a candy, this is a pleasant change from after-dinner mints and may also be nibbled as a breath freshener or used as an edible cake decoration.

¼ lb. $1.35
1 lb. $4.70

Coriander Seeds

In the *Arabian Nights* tales, coriander is spoken of as an ingredient in love potions. Today, it is mainly a cooking condiment, one of the basic ingredients in curry powder and Indian cooking.

¼ lb. $.75
1 lb. $2.25

Cream of Tartar

A natural fruit derivative made from powdered grapes, cream of tartar is used in making candies, frostings, and beaten egg whites.

¼ lb. $1.75
1 lb. $6.15

Curry Powder

This well-known spice blend can be used to make "curries" or to flavor a variety of other foods. It is often used in egg dishes, or with meat, fish, cooked vegetables, and even breads. The types of curry powder that are already blended are:

Medium Hot Indian Curry Powder
¼ lb. $.95 1 lb. $3.30
Extra Hot Curry Powder ¼ lb. $1.15
1 lb. $3.95
Malaysian Curry Powder 4-oz. tin
$1.15
Jamaican Curry Powder ¼ lb. $1.15
1 lb. $3.95

Cumin Seed

This fragrant seed is essential in Mexican, Indian, and Middle Eastern cooking. Cumin is especially good in yogurt dishes, salads, dips.

Whole: ¼ lb. $1.35
1 lb. $4.70
Ground: ¼ lb. $1.55
1 lb. $5.50

Dandelion Leaf

The most common of garden pests, dandelion is also known as *priest's crown* and *swine's snout*. Dandelion leaves make a deliciously bitter tea. You can also use them in omelets, soups, breads, jellies, puddings. A natural dye, dandelion leaves will turn a fabric a deep magenta.

¼ lb. $1.15
1 lb. $8.00

Dill Seed

Called the "meetinghouse" seed by American colonists, dill was nibbled to prevent hunger while spending long hours in church. Dill seed is often used in conjunction with mint in Middle Eastern dishes and adds zest to rice, fish, breads.

¼ lb. $.75
1 lb. $2.50

Dill Weed

In the Middle Ages, a bit of dill weed was believed to enhance passion. Today it is used mainly as a cooking condiment and is very common in Middle Eastern and Scandinavian cooking.

¼ lb. $2.65
1 lb. $9.30

Fennel Seed

A symbol of heroism, it is also called *sweet fennel*. A tea made from these seeds is said to aid in controlling the appetite. Try fennel seeds in puddings, sausages, cakes, pickles, liqueurs.

Whole: ¼ lb. $.95
1 lb. $3.30
Ground: ¼ lb. $1.15
1 lb. $3.95

Five Spices Powder, Chinese

A pungent, sweet-smelling blend of cinnamon, fennel, star anise, cloves, and Szechuan pepper, this powder has a strong licoricelike taste. It is especially good (used sparingly) in pork, chicken, and duck dishes.

¼ lb. $2.35
1 lb. $8.25

Garlic

A popular cooking condiment, minced garlic is much stronger than garlic powder.

Minced garlic: ¼ lb. $1.35
1 lb. $4.70
Garlic powder (100% pure garlic):
¼ lb. $1.35
1 lb. $4.70

Ginger, Wild

This is native to North America and is also known as *Indian berry* and

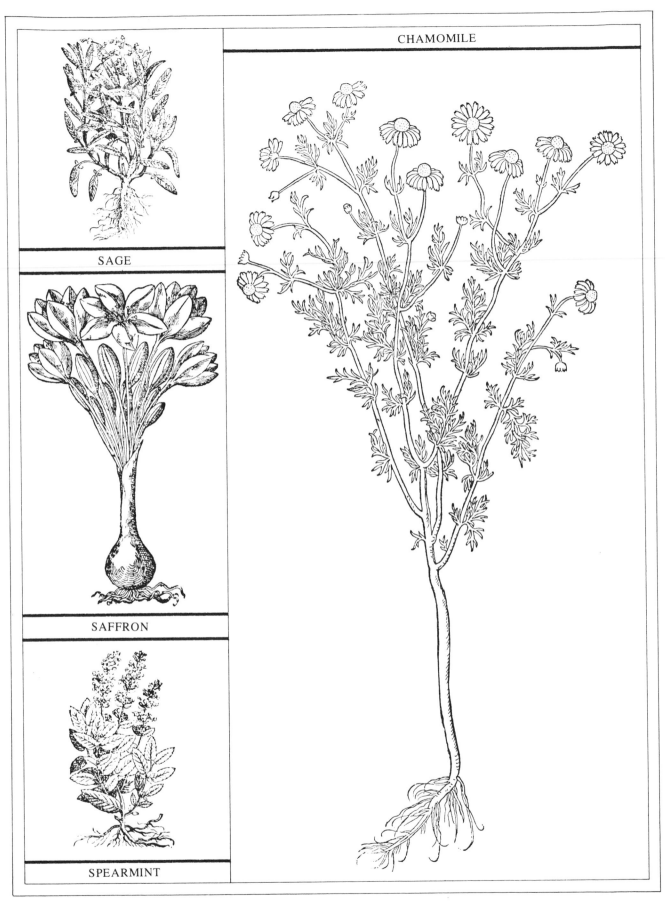

CHAMOMILE

SAGE

SAFFRON

SPEARMINT

Canadian snakeroot. Wild ginger is usually brewed into a tea, and good when made together with orange peel.

¼ lb. $2.60
1 lb. $8.00

Ginger

This well-known spice is actually the rhizome of a plant indigenous to South Asia. The best-quality ginger is now grown in Jamaica. Ground ginger adds zest to chutneys and soups. Whole dried ginger root is often brewed into tea or used to make "freshly ground" ginger powder. Whole fresh ginger root is frequently used in Chinese and Indian cooking.

Ginger root:
¼ lb. $1.35
1 lb. $4.70

Lemon Peel

Lemon peel is used in cakes, breads, cookies, sauces, potpourris, sachets.

¼ lb. $1.75
1 lb. $6.15

Lemon Verbena

The Spanish call it *Yerba Louisa* and brew it into tea. In France, it is brewed into the popular Vervaine tisane. Powdered and mixed with salt, lemon verbena is popular in Turkish cooking. Or use it in soups, jellies, jams.

¼ lb. $2.65
1 lb. $9.30

Licorice Root

Chew on the root instead of candy—it has helped many people stop smoking and contains no sugar. Brew licorice into a tea, and it will sweeten the brew naturally.

¼ lb. $1.15
1 lb. $3.95

Marjoram

Also known as *sweet marjoram,* this was a symbol of happiness to the ancient Greeks. Marjoram is closely related to oregano and is often used in herbal blends such as bouquet garni, poultry seasonings, and the like.

¼ lb. $1.25
1 lb. $4.25

Mustard Seeds

Black mustard seeds are an important ingredient in Indian cooking. Yellow mustard seeds are the more common variety. They are used in pickles, relishes, salads, spiced meats, curries.

Black: ¼ lb. $.75
1 lb. $2.50
Yellow: ¼ lb. $.55
1 lb. $2.00

Mustard Powder

This is made from ground yellow mustard seeds. For an English-type mustard, just add water. For the Chinese variety, use vinegar and a little salt. Often spices and herbs are added.

¼ lb. $.55
1 lb. $2.00

Nutmeg

The finest East Indian nutmeg has an exotic sweet taste, which is quite strong. Try a bit grated into a cup of

tea or coffee; use in soufflés, cream sauces, pies, cakes.

Whole: ¼ lb. $1.95
1 lb. $6.85
Ground: ¼ lb. $2.05
1 lb. $7.10

Orange Peel

Orange peel is used in breads, cakes, candies, sachets, potpourris, teas.

¼ lb. $1.15
1 lb. $3.95

Oregano

Sometimes called *wild marjoram,* this is essential in Italian and Mexican cooking. Delicious in almost all types of dishes except sweet ones, and particularly good in spaghetti and pizza sauces. Cosmetically, oregano can be used in mouthwashes, salves, liniment. It also makes an invigorating tea.

¼ lb. $1.45
1 lb. $5.00

Orris Root

Whole orris root is also known as *love root* or *Queen Elizabeth root.* Chopped or powdered orris root is a popular fixative in pomanders, potpourris, and sachets.

¼ lb. $2.65
1 lb. $9.30

Papaya Leaves

These leaves are usually brewed into a tea, alone or with mint added.

¼ lb. $1.55
1 lb. $5.50

Parsley

The ancient Greeks and Romans ate parsley after eating garlic and onions, to remove odors from their breath. It really works. Parsley is also used as a flavoring and garnish in soups, salads, meat, egg dishes.

¼ lb. $1.55
1 lb. $5.50

Paprika

A native of the Western Hemisphere, paprika is a mild ground spice of the Capsicum family. Spanish paprika is the most common variety in the United States. It is used mainly as a "garnish" spice, giving a bright red color.

¼ lb. $.95
1 lb. $3.30

Peppercorns

Black peppercorns from Lampong, India, can be bought either whole or ground. Black peppercorns from Tellicherry, India, are the finest-quality peppercorns grown. They are bigger, darker, more pungent than any others. Green peppercorns are packed in water and add an elegant gourmet touch in French cooking. Add to prepared mustard, use in dips, spreads. White peppercorns from Muntok, India, are sharp and pungent. The French especially favor using them. They blend better in cream sauces, etc.

Black peppercorns, Lampong, India
¼ lb. $.75 1 lb. $2.50
Black peppercorns, Tellicherry, India ¼ lb. $1.10 1 lb. $3.85
Green peppercorns 3½ oz. $2.95
White peppercorns ¼ lb. $1.35 1 lb. $4.70

Peppers

Cayenne powdered red pepper, very hot. Crushed red peppers, very hot. Can be used on pizza or in Mexican food. Szechuan Chinese anise pepper is usually used together with star anise in "red cooked" dishes and marinades.

Cayenne pepper ¼ lb. $1.35
Crushed red peppers ¼ lb. $.95
Szechuan pepper ¼ lb. $2.10

Peppermint

More biting than any other mint, this is used mainly in beverages and sweets.

¼ lb. $1.55
1 lb. $5.50

Pickling Spice

This is a popular combination of spices used in making pickles, relishes, and also in sauerkraut dishes.

¼ lb. $.55
1 lb. $1.95

Pine Nuts (Pignoli)

Used in Middle Eastern and Italian cooking, they are especially good in rice dishes, stuffed grape leaves, and cookies.

¼ lb. $1.75
1 lb. $6.85

Poppy Seeds

There are approximately 900,000 of these tiny blue-black seeds in each pound. They have a mild nutlike flavor and are used in cakes, pastries, on breads and rolls, or added to buttered noodles or salads.

¼ lb. $.60
1 lb. $2.10

Poppy Seeds, White

This variety of poppy seeds is often used in Indian cooking.

¼ lb. $1.45
1 lb. $5.00

Quinine Bark

Also known as *Peruvian bark,* this is used in hair tonics.

¼ lb. $1.15
1 lb. $6.15

Raspberries, Dried

These are delicious in hot tea during the cold weather, one or two raspberries to each cup. Add a few to Brandy to flavor it.

¼ lb. $1.45
1 lb. $5.00

Rosehips

These are the fruit of the wild rose plant. They make a deliciously tart tea and are also good in jams and preserves. They are an excellent source of vitamin C.

Crushed rosehips without seeds
¼ lb. $1.55, 1 lb. $5.50
Crushed rosehips with seeds (for tea)
¼ lb. $1.15, 1 lb. $3.95
Whole rosehips (for tea) ¼ lb. $.95, 1 lb. $3.30

Rosemary

The symbol of remembrance and friendship, it is used mainly as a pungent and delightful cooking herb. Rosemary is used with lamb, chicken, shrimp, breads, vegetables, stuffing, fruit (especially citrus fruit), salads.

¼ lb. $1.15
1 lb. $3.95

Rosemary, Wild

Wild rosemary has an earthier taste than the garden variety and adds an interesting difference to wild game dishes.

¼ lb. $1.35
1 lb. $4.70

Saffron

This is true Spanish saffron. The most delicate of spices, saffron comes from the stigma of a very special crocus. Used in Spanish paella, bouillabaisse, and many other gourmet dishes.

2/5 gram $1.50
1 gram $2.95

Sage

Garden sage is an ancient symbol of wisdom. It is commonly used in stuffings, sauces, soups, stews, herb cheese.

¼ lb. $.95
1 lb. $3.30

Shallots

A mild member of the onion family, shallots are an essential in fine French cooking. Use in salads or chopped and sprinkled on steaks.

½ oz. $1.10
1 oz. $2.00
¼ lb. $7.50

Sesame Seeds

These tiny seeds are very prevalent in Middle Eastern cookery or sprinkled on top of Italian breads.

¼ lb. $.40
1 lb. $1.25

Spearmint

Garden mint, lamb mint, or green mint is often brewed into an invigorating tea. Spearmint is much used in the Middle East in cooking, and in Europe in mint sauces.

¼ lb. $1.35
1 lb. $4.70

Strawberry Leaves

A symbol of foresight, from which a refreshing tea is often made, strawberry leaves can be brewed alone or with other herbs such as woodruff. Good in cold drinks and soothing in baths.

¼ lb. $1.35
1 lb. $4.70

Tarragon

A warmly aromatic and slightly biting condiment herb, this is used to make tarragon vinegar and Bearnaise sauce.

¼ lb. $2.15
1 lb. $7.55

Thyme, Wild

Also known as *mother of thyme*, it has a bold, heady scent and can be used in cooking or brewed into tea.

¼ lb. $1.35
1 lb. $4.70

Thyme

A symbol of courage. A pinch of thyme is a necessary ingredient in Manhattan clam chowder and is also good in other soups, stews, stuffings, salad dressings, fish, and most vegetables.

¼ lb. $.75
1 lb. $2.50

Tumeric

This is the bright yellow ingredient in curry powder. It is also used commercially in prepared mustards. Many people use tumeric to add color to yellow rice dishes. Good, too, in curries, pickles, relishes.

¼ lb. $.85
1 lb. $3.00

Vanilla Bean

Native to Mexico, this bean was brought to Europe by the Spanish conquerors. The bean is the fruit of an orchid plant and is used for flavoring ice cream, puddings, cakes.

4 for $1.00

Vanillin

A white powder that gives a rich vanilla taste, it is used by most professional bakers.

½ oz. $1.35
1 oz. $2.40
¼ lb. $8.40

The Mail-Order Food Book

7.

Cod

Cured in the traditional way handed down by seafarers for 300 years, the "just-caught" goodness of the cod fillets is preserved as it comes to port from a North Atlantic fishing fleet. Each wooden pail contains 5 pounds net weight of choice fillets of salt cod. The same fine fillets are also available in a smaller edition. Packed in a 2-pound paper Kraft box, they are ideal for a family meal.

5-lb. pail $15.00
2-lb. box $5.95

Embassy Seafoods

Maine Codfish

From Maine you can order a tub of real Maine salt codfish. Every fillet is carefully selected and packed in a tub. Comes complete with easy-do cooking and eating directions.

1 tub $15.95

Crawford Lobster Company

Codfish Cakes

This is the heart of a sturdy Yankee breakfast. Embassy has combined their salt cod fluff with their own choice ingredients to make an authentic New England codfish cake. Each can makes from four to six generous cakes. Use it as is, or add to corn-fritter batter. Its uses are unlimited.

3 10½-oz. cans $3.50
6 10½-oz. cans $6.50

Embassy Seafoods

Finnan Haddie

Creamed Finnan Haddie is made from fine imported fish and packed in a rich buttery cream sauce. Comes in cans that are ready to heat and serve on toast points at a moment's notice.

3 15-oz. cans $4.95
6 15-oz. cans $9.90

Embassy Seafoods

Gefilte Fish

Delicate baby carp are used in the preparation of this traditional specialty. The stuffing is an aromatic blend of pure fresh spices, garden vegetables, and eggs. There is nothing artificial to mar its subtle taste.

10½-oz. tin $1.98
6 tins $11.00
12 tins $20.00
Case of 50 tins $80.00

Paprikas Weiss

Iceland Seafood

This food package includes smoked lamb, cheese spreads (plain and with shrimps), lamp paté, lamb's liver paté, lamb's cheek, brook trout, shrimps, lumpfish caviar, herring tidbits in wine sauce, kipper snacks.

Assortment above $24.50 including air mail postage

Icemart

Icelandic Seafood Package

From Iceland, famous for its seafood and one of the world's major fish-exporting nations, you can now sample shrimps, lumpfish caviar, cod roes, kipper snacks, cod-liver paté, brook trout, brisling-sardines, capelin.

Assortment above $14.95 including airmail postage

Icemart

Mixed Seafood

Antipasto (Italy)	3½-oz. jar	$1.40
Boneless Scotch Kippers	7-oz. tin	1.50
Fancy Canadian Lobster	4-oz. tin	6.95
Fancy Crab Meat	7¾-oz. tin	5.95
Fancy Royal Chinook Salmon	7¾-oz. tin	2.50
Gefilte Fish (Israel)	10½-oz. tin	1.95
Quenelles de Brochet au Natural	9-oz. tin	1.95
Rainbow Trout (smoked halves)	8-oz. tin	4.25
Smoked Mussels	3½-oz. tin	1.75
Smoked Oysters (Bendicksens)	3¼-oz. jar	1.95
Smoked Sturgeon	3¼-oz. jar	1.75

Maison Glass

Mackerel

Selected choice mackerel fillets are packed in a reusable wooden bucket with brine and pure white table salt. Broil, bake, or boil to suit your taste. Each one of the 12 plump mackerel in the pail weighs nearly a pound and provides a gourmet treat for three people.

5-lb. pail $12.00
10-lb. pail $24.00

Embassy Seafoods

Maine Salt Mackerel

These real Maine Salt Mackerel fillets are carefully selected and packed in tubs for shipment. Easy-do cooking and eating directions are sent with each tub.

1 tub $12.50. Add $1.50 west of Mississippi

Crawford Lobster Company

Red Snapper

Considered by many as the most prized fish for eating, this red snapper has firm white meat and delicate flavor. A ''plus'' is the special crabmeat stuffing that makes it a specialty of the house. Comes completely prepared for baking or broiling and will serve six to eight people.

4 snappers with crabmeat stuffing $35.95

R. H. Chamberlin

St. Peter's Fish

This is the species tradition has it that St. Peter caught in the Sea of Galilee centuries ago. Now raised indoors in pollution-free waters and fed on a diet of selected vegetables, St. Peter's Fish is the product of a new fish-growing concept. The result is a mild, tasty, fork-tender fish low in calories and cholesterol. Thaw, then bake, broil, or fry in just a few minutes. Cooking instructions come with order.

8 6- to 8-oz. fillets $27.50
12 6- to 8-oz. fillets $35.00

Omaha Steaks International

Salmon Canned in Glass

This is a unqiue glass-canned edition of natural Alaska salmon. Choice, fresh fish—Kings, Reds, and Medium Reds—are processed in season. The fish are skinned, boned, filleted, and hand-packed in glass jars. It bears little resemblance to salmon canned in tin. The flesh is firm as it comes from the jar and great for use in salads or casseroles.

12 5-oz. jars $13.96. Postage $3.90
24 5-oz. jars $27.44. Postage $6.24
48 5-oz. jars $52.96. Postage $10.86

Briggs-Way Company

Sardines

Delicious sardines are packed in soybean oil or with soybean oil and hot green chilies. Specify which you prefer.

12-oz. can $.75

Especially Maine

Imported Sardines

These imported sardines from Norway and Portugal are packed in olive oil.

Brisling (Norway) 3¾ oz. tin $1.25
Boneless and Skinless Sardines (Portugal) 3¾ oz. tin $1.25
7 oz. tin $2.25

Maison Glass

Seafood in the Round

A wide range of Northwest favorites are cleverly packed in a round reed basket encased with a fish net. Contains Alder Smoked butter clams, smoked sturgeon, smoked salmon, smoked albacore, tuna, and tiny North Pacific shrimp meat.

1 basket $5.95

Hegg and Hegg

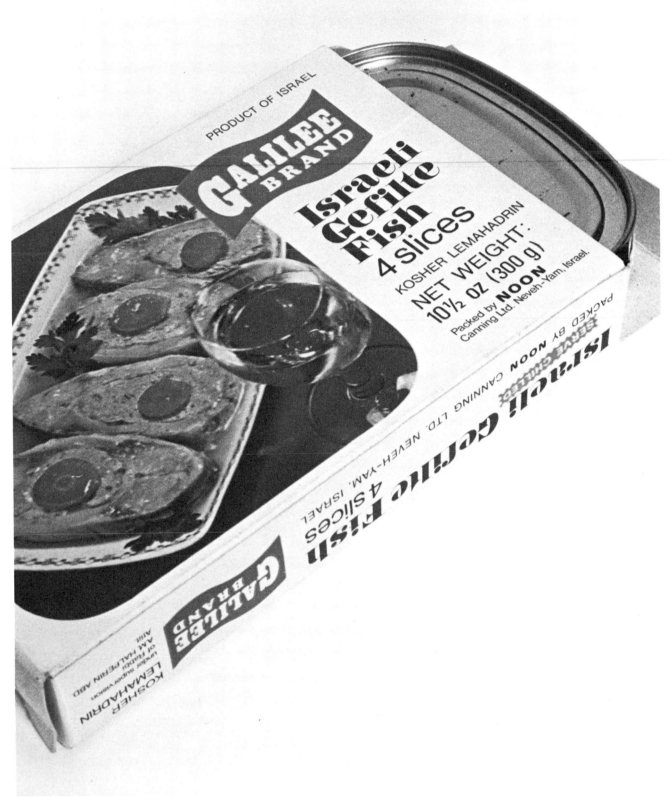

Shad Roe

Two whole roes of shad roe add up to a true delicacy.

7-oz. tin $4.50

Maison Glass

Embassy Shad Roe

Each can of Embassy brand shad roe contains the finest obtainable roes. After careful inspection of each lobe for excellent quality and condition, the roes are partially precooked and seasoned with salt to preserve that "right from the ocean" flavor.

3 7¾-oz. cans $17.50
6 7¾-oz. cans $35.00

Embassy Seafoods

Shore Dinners

These taste-tempting Florida Seafood menus feature a novel shrimp ring or delicate blue-crab appetizer, pre-cooked lobsters, stone crab claws or rock shrimp entrees, and a rich and tangy homemade Florida Key lime pie. Shore Dinners serve six people.

Lobster (No. 651) $41.95
Stone crab claws (No. 652) $51.95
Red snapper (No. 654) $40.95
Rock shrimp (No. 653) $41.95

R. H. Chamberlin

Surf and Turf

A combination dinner treat that offers specially prepared and precooked Florida Lobster halves stuffed with crabmeat dressing *plus* fork-tender filet mignon aged to perfection. Serves four people.

4 lobster halves with stuffing plus 4 6-oz. steaks $41.95

R. H. Chamberlin

Steamed Clams in the Shell

These are young, tender, juicy steamed clams—a true New England delight. One dozen or more come in each can. Serve with melted butter and the natural juices from the can.

3 cans $3.10
6 cans $6.05

Embassy Seafoods

Clam Dip

Choice chopped clams, cream cheese, Sherry, and other fine ingredients are blended in an exclusive recipe.

3 6-oz. cans $2.75
6 6-oz. cans $4.95

Embassy Seafoods

Florida Stone Crab Claws

These aristocrats of the Florida seas offer a taste treat to pamper royalty. Their flavor and size will stamp you a seafood connoisseur among your friends. Precooked, you just heat them and serve. Six pounds of claws will serve four to six people.

6 lb. $43.95
10 lb. $56.50

R. H. Chamberlin

Frozen Florida Stone Crab Claws

A treat that is elegant to serve and entertaining as well. Just heat them or serve cold. They have been cooked immediately when caught, to preserve their succulent flavor. Seldom available outside of fine Florida restaurants, they are shipped fresh frozen from Florida November through August.

6 lb. $44.50
8 lb. $55.00

Omaha Steaks International

King Crabmeat

As each king crab is caught, it is processed aboard superbly equipped fishing ships. Each can contains 7½ ounces of choicest American crabmeat, boned and hand-picked to reduce fragmentation. Write supplier for current prices.

Embassy Seafoods

Maine Crabmeat

Here are parchment-lined tins of "feather-free" Maine crab. The crisp, flavorful meat is ready to serve in salads or sandwiches.

4 6-oz. tins $18.95

Saltwater Farm

Fresh Florida Lobster

The finest lobsters from Florida's abundant Atlantic and Caribbean waters are expertly prepared and precooked to seal in the superb "fresh-from-the-sea" flavor. Ready to heat, serve, and enjoy.

4 lobsters (8 halves) average live wt. 1⅓ lb. $37.95

R. H. Chamberlin

Live Lobsters

Hard-shelled Maine lobsters are shipped from Cap'n Crawford's in a self-cooking container plus a quart of real sea water to cook them in. The water ensures that real authentic flavor. All shipments go air freight and are given special handling until they arrive at your airport. Complete cooking and eating directions precede each shipment.

6 1-lb. lobsters $37.95
12 1-lb. lobsters $66.95

Crawford Lobster Company

Lobster Dip

This is a superb mixture of lobster meat, lobster butter, cream cheese, Sherry, and other fine ingredients.

3 6-oz. cans $3.15
6 6-oz. cans $6.15

Embassy Seafoods

Lobster Meat

This is the prize of the icy North Atlantic—the choicest meat of young chicken lobsters from Gloucester Bay to the Bay of Fundy. Each can contains only tender, solid, pink-white lobster meat. Unconditionally guaranteed to be of excellent quality or your money back.

3 5-oz. cans $16.85
6 5-oz. cans $32.50

Embassy Seafoods

Live Lobsters

All Saltwater Farm lobsterbakes are shipped to your nearest airport in a metal steaming container inside a specially designed, reusable polystyrene shipping container. The outer container makes a perfect party-size ice bucket for later. All live seafood from Saltwater Farm carries a warranty of replacement, equivalent credit, or refund in the unlikely event that an order fails to arrive in prime shape or before the date specified.

Quantity	Regular	Quarters	Selects	Jumbos
4	$ 31.00	$ 32.00	$ 37.50	$ 54.60
6	38.25	43.95	52.75	79.05
8	47.70	57.95	68.95	103.40
10	58.50	70.45	85.15	131.50
12	69.30	83.65	101.35	156.75
14	80.10	96.95	117.55	180.00
16	90.90	115.45	133.75	203.50
18	100.50	127.45	149.95	231.75
20	112.50	138.50	165.00	257.00

Saltwater Farm

Lobster Newburg

This is really special and absolutely delicious with plenty of lobster in luscious creamy sauce.

3 10½-oz. cans $13.00
6 10½-oz. cans $26.00

Embassy Seafoods

Gourmet Lobster Tails

A seafood treasure is imported for your delight from lobster beds half a world away. They are firm white meat grown to a superior flavor and pleasing fork-tender texture in clear, turbulent waters. Easy cooking and serving instructions come with order.

8 6- to 8-oz. tails $48.00

Omaha Steaks International

Maine Lobster Tails

With unsurpassable flavor, these tails come from pound-and-a-quarter (or larger) lobsters and are packed to arrive deep frozen and ready for use.

12 (minimum 4 oz.) $35.50
20 (minimum 4 oz.) $55.50

Saltwater Farm

Petite Lobster Tails

These lobster tails actually match the delicate flavor and texture of larger tails. They are equally tasty and tender—and they accommodate every size of appetite. Easy cooking and serving instructions come with order.

20 1½- to 2-oz. tails $34.00

Omaha Steaks International

Rock Shrimp

These shrimp are tender, succulent, and a subtle combination of the flavors of lobster and shrimp. Follow the recipe enclosed with your order, serve in the shell, and have a "triumphant" dinner. Guaranteed to arrive deep frozen.

4 lb. $41.05
6 lb. $48.90
8 lb. $55.85

Saltwater Farm

Rock Shrimp

These scarce, deep-water seafood delicacies with the distinctive baked or broiled lobster-shrimp flavor are a rare dining treat. Arrive completely prepared and ready for easy cooking. Four pounds serve six people.

4 lb. $37.95
6 lb. $44.50
8 lb. $50.95

R. H. Chamberlin

Shrimp Dip

Plump shrimp, cream cheese, and Sherry combine to provide just the right texture and flavor. A "must" for the pantry shelf.

3 6-oz. cans $2.75
6 6-oz. cans $4.95

Embassy Seafoods

SMOKED SALMON

Alder Smoked Salmon

Alder Smoked Salmon is choice, specially selected red salmon, full of the fresh sea tang of the famous Puget Sound fishing grounds. Smoked by an exclusive process that is not a "hard" but a "soft" smoke that retains all the delicate texture of fresh salmon plus the delicious flavor of rich Alder Smoke. Comes vacuum sealed in a plastic container that will keep for long periods under normal refrigeration. After package is opened, smoked salmon keeps under refrigeration for a week; for longer storage freezing is necessary.

Approx. 4 lb. whole salmon $14.25 half salmon $8.00

Hegg and Hegg

Irish Smoked Salmon

Firm, smoked to perfection, and cured to an uncompromising exactness, these salmon from the sparkling northern waters of Ireland assure fresh flavor and easy-to-slice firmness. Omaha selects only the finest and prepares them with their traditional artistry for curing and smoking. Shipped October through March.

2-lb. minimum side $24.75

Omaha Steaks International

Irish Smoked Salmon

All ready to slice and serve, this salmon has been flown from Ireland for immediate shipment. It has excellent keeping qualities, and any unused portions can be refrozen without damage to its taste or texture.

1 side $23.50
2 sides shipped to same address $43.55
10 or more sides shipped to any addresses in continental U.S. $21.15 per side

Saltwater Farm

Scottish Highlands Salmon

Ritchie Brothers use salmon taken from Scottish Highland rivers and

The Mail-Order Food Book

smoke it in their own kilns on the Island-of-Bute. They use an ABC cure (Authentic Bland Cure) that brings out the natural flavor of the salmon. The fish are cured for two days and two nights and then smoked for one night over oak shavings. No artificial flavoring or color is used.

2-lb. slab side $26.00

Ritchie Brothers

Smoked Salmon Caviar Spread

This is a salt-preserved pasteurized product made from salmon eggs. The similarity to caviar ends there, for it tastes more like smoked salmon than caviar. The salmon eggs are delicately flavored by smoking with natural hickory smoke seasoned with natural garlic powder and pepper sauce before processing. As this spread is nearly 30 percent protein it is nourishing as well as delicious.

4 2½-oz. jars $8.48. Postage $1.88
6 2½-oz. jars $12.58. Postage $2.14
12 2½-oz. jars $24.58. Postage $3.12
24 2½-oz. jars $49.98. Postage $4.36

Briggs-Way Company

Smoked Salmon and Cheddar Spread

The salmon and cheddar combine to make a mouth-watering spread for sandwiches, snacks, and canapés.

3 2½-oz. cans $2.10
6 2½-oz. cans $4.00

Embassy Seafoods

Escargot (Snails)

This assortment contains a tin of 24 snails with shells, a snail seasoning, a package of plates, and two French holders and forks.

Assortment above $22.50

Maison Glass

Imported Snails

With shells. 24 in box $7.95
Without shells. 24 in can $4.25

Lekvar By The Barrel

Tins of Snails

Size	Quantity	Price
Regular	12	$ 2.10
Extra large	18	3.45
Regular	24	4.10
Extra large	24	4.55
Extra large	36	6.65
Regular	48	8.25
Colossal	60	12.00
Extra large	72	13.20
Regular	96	16.00

Le Jardin du Gourmet

8.

DRIED AND TINNED FRUITS

Apricots, Plums, Dates

All are softly steamed to make them plump and succulent. They never dry out and will keep for months. Australian apricots are huge, tender halves from specialty orchards "down under." Candied, and chock full of sass and flavor. French plums are hand-pitted, steamed, and plumped to flavorful, natural perfection—super on a salad plate. Medjool dates are costly but worth every cent. All three come packed in a handsome handmade pine crate and are available between November 10 and May 15.

Order Gift No. 376 $12.95 delivered

Harry and David

Blueberries

They say that "blueberries grow sweetest in Maine." Enjoy these beauties year-round. They come tinned and with Sarah Wyman's recipes for pie and muffins on the label.

14 oz. packed in syrup $.85
14 oz. packed in water $.75

Especially Maine

About Dates

Dates are the fruit of the date palm tree, perhaps the oldest cultivated tree. Next to the coconut palm, the date palm is the most interesting and useful of the palm family. Its fruit is as nourishing as wheat or corn flour, and when treated and stuffed with nuts or paste, dates turn into exquisite confections.

Deglet Noor, or "Date of Light," originated in the oases of Algeria. This long, amber, naturally firm date has a distinctive flavor and is excellent for stuffing. It is not as sweet as most dates but is an excellent keeper.

Zahidi, which means "of small quantity," or "nobility," is a

medium-sized golden yellow date that originated in northern Iraq. Like the Deglet Noor, it is a semidry date and an excellent keeper.

Medjool, one of the choicest dates in the Mediterranean area, no longer exists in the Old World. A large, attractive, soft delicious date with an excellent quality that ships and keeps well, Medjool has been referred to as the "perfect date."

Halawy offshoots were first imported in the United States in commercial quantity from Basra, Iraq, in 1913. They were considered the best date variety shipped from that area, and are second in the number of palms in southern Iraq. This long, slender, light amber date is soft and sweet, which is the meaning of the name.

In shape, *Barhi* is almost round; it is amber to mahogany brown in color when ripe. The flesh is thick, smooth, and soft, and the flavor is rich and delicate. This is an exceptionally fine date that was not shipped until recently because of its softness. Now, by refrigerating the dates immediately after picking, then letting them cure down before picking, they can be shipped safely. The Barhi's superb quality is the standard by which all other dates are judged.

Khadrawy means "green," referring to either the greenish cast of the fruit as it begins to soften or to the bright green foliage of the gracefully arching leaf midribs.

Organic dates are grown in the deep virgin soil of an ancient sea bed—120 acres—and are maintained by true organic soil building for 30 years. No poisonous dusts or sprays are used on organic date palms, and no chemical preservative mars the flavor of the dates.

Medjhul Dates

These gigantic dates—about twice the size of ordinary dates—are deliciously sweet, moist but firm—and not sticky. They're so huge and so tasty that your friends will be amazed and delighted. Order for gifts or for yourself.

Gift Box (30 dates) $7.05
Home Tin (90 dates) $15.30
Case of 7 Gift Boxes shipped to one address $40.25

Sunnyland Farms

Medjool Dates

Grown in one of California's desert gardens, these dates are as delicious as their impressive size—about three times the size of an ordinary date (16 to 23 per pound).

2 lbs. $10.75

C. C. Graber Co.

Smyrna Figs

Plucked from the fabled fig trees of biblical stories, these are plump, meaty fruits, sweet with their own natural sugars.

1 lb. $2.98
3 1-lb. packages $8.00
6 1-lb. packages $15.00

Paprikas Weiss

Fruit Basket

A choice selection of fancy dried fruits in an attractive arrangement. Basket includes dates, figs, apricots, pears, prunes, pineapple, glacéed cherries, and walnuts.

1½ lb. $6.95
3 lb. $10.95

Figi's

Stuffed California Dates

Stuffed with:	1-lb. Price
Almond paste	$4.20
Assorted nuts	4.50
Cashews	4.10
Pecans	4.35
Variety nuts	4.60
Walnuts	3.70
Walnuts and almond paste (half 'n' half)	4.10
Walnuts and pecans (half 'n' half)	4.10

Pete's California Dates

Dried Fruits

Item	Quantity and Size		Unit Price	Price
Apples (Family Orchard brand)	12	4 oz.	$ .57	$ 6.84
Apricots (Family Orchard brand)	12	6 oz.	1.06	12.76
Chinese Red Pitted Dates	10	8 oz.	.35	3.50
Deglect Noor Dates	12	16 oz.	1.00	12.00
Giant Red Bananas (Green Earth brand)	12	3 oz.	.40	4.80
Large Brook Prunes (Sunray brand)	12	16 oz.	.82	9.84
Large Italian Prunes (Sunray brand)	12	16 oz.	.78	9.36
Mixed Fruit	12	12 oz.	1.14	13.68
Peaches (Family Orchard brand)	12	6 oz.	.84	10.08
Pears (Family Orchard brand)	12	8 oz.	.80	9.60
Pineapple (Timbercrest brand)	12	8 oz.	1.17	14.04

Erewhon

Fruit Buffet

This is 1½ pounds of moist and luscious fruit treats—including Calimyrna figs, whole dates, confectionized French plums, and tangy apricots—some of them topped with nuts. A veritable smorgasbord of nature's finest snacks in a handy reusable wicker serving tray. Great to have on hand for last-minute gifts—and guests.

Order Gift No. 375 $8.95 delivered

Harry and David

Fruit Tray

The biggest, finest, plumpest dates, date and nut rolls, figs and walnuts, prunes with almonds and apricots. After the fruit is gone, the tray makes a handy serving piece.

Net wt. 1 lb. 6 oz. $5.95

The Swiss Colony

Fruit Pac Honey Dipped Dried Fruit

A healthful confection, organically grown without the use of sprays or chemicals. Fruit Pac brand dried fruits are distinguished by being honey dipped, which means that they are preserved with natural honey instead of with synthetic chemicals.

	1-lb. Price
Dates	$1.36
Breakfast prunes	1.13
Jumbo prunes	1.36
Large prunes	1.17
Monukka raisins	1.49
Thompson raisins	1.50

Rancher Waltenspiel

Prunes

Prunes from the Sunray Orchards in Oregon are washed in well and spring water, then dried in hot-air dehydrators to preserve their maximum flavor and texture. The tenderizing process goes on throughout the year, so the prunes are always fresh. No preservatives or mold inhibitors are used, and the careful preparation ensures that the prunes are never "overprocessed." The Sunray people are prune specialists. Prunes are their only commodity—a very delicious one. Many varieties are available; send for price list of individual varieties.

FRESH FRUITS

Crisp Mountain Apples

These apples are raised way up North in the cold country where they get crackling crisp and snappy. Each one weighs better than half a pound and measures over three inches in diameter.

Order Gift No. 23 over 7½ lb. $9.95
Order Gift No. 20 (twice as much fruit as No. 23) $17.95
Order Gift No. 95 (6 lb. apples with

6 1-lb. bags, premium sizes ("Gift Box") $5.00

Sunray Orchards

Stuffed Fruit

The fruits of antiquity—dates, figs, prunes, apricots—dried or stuffed with delicious fruit blends, such as Calimyrna figs filled with a blend of peaches, pears, lemon juice, honey, and walnuts. Packed in a rattan tray.

1 lb. $8.75
1½ lb. $11.95

Pepperidge Farm

a ¾-lb. brick prime Cheddar cheese) $11.95

Harry and David

Shenandoah Valley Apples

From the famous Shenandoah Valley of Virginia you can get a "poison-free apple"—one that is organically grown. They are supreme in nutritional value and a tangy, spicy joy to bite into. Apples grown in this region, often referred to as the Apple Capital of America, are famed for their excellence.

One tray packed Bushel Box at the farm $10.75
¼ bushel shipped $4.95, $5.55, $5.95.
1 bushel shipped $14.25, $15.25, $16.75
(Prices vary according to delivery area.)

Golden Acres Orchard

Vermont Fine Native Apples

These apples are nurtured by warm sunny days and made shiny red and juicy by crisp Vermont nights. They are picked tenderly by hand during

the cool autumn days and packed in specially designed gift boxes with great care. McIntosh, Cortland, Northern Spy, and Red Delicious come in the apple packs.

7 lb. (15-apple pack) $3.95
14 lb. (30-apple pack) $7.25
21 lb. (45-apple pack) $10.50
9 lb. Bennington Box $10.15
9 lb. Ethan Allen Box $7.45
9 lb. Vermont Box $8.70

Harwood Hill Orchard

Avocado

This is the fruit that makes salads a memorable occasion. If you wish, you can order half-avocado and half-mango shipments at the same prices shown below.

½ lug $8.95
Full lug $14.95
½ bushel $19.95

R. H. Chamberlin

Citrus Fruit Assortments

Citrus fruits from Chamberlin come from their own and other famous groves, including the renowned groves of Indian River. Every orange and grapefruit is picked by hand at the pinnacle of perfection and is sorted, washed, and polished by the most modern techniques. No artificial coloring or flavor is ever added. This top-quality Florida citrus is rushed by special trucks directly to any address in the continental U.S. (except Alaska, Arizona, Hawaii) and Canada. Or it will be flown by jet to Europe.

Champagne Hamper—a sturdy handwoven import gift for special friends. All fruit or deluxe packed.
½ bushel $21.95
1 bushel   28.95
½ bushel deluxe   26.95
1 bushel deluxe   32.95

Tropical Palmbo—a bright and colorful gift basket of many uses. All fruit or deluxe packed:
½ bushel $16.98
⁴/₅ bushel   22.95
½ bushel deluxe   20.95
⁴/₅ bushel deluxe   27.95

R. H. Chamberlin

Deluxe Plus

Vitamin-packed seedless grapefruit and sun-sweet navels, tangelos, and temple oranges are packed with honey, jellies, marmalades, and a crunchy fresh pecan log for an abundance of flavorful eating.

½ bushel $15.45
¾ bushel $18.45
1 bushel $21.45

Harvey's Groves

Fruit Buffet

Moist and luscious fruit treats including Calimyrna figs, big whole dates, confectionized French plums, and tangy apricots. Some are topped with nuts.

1½ lb. $8.95

Harry and David

Fruit-of-the-Month Club

3 box gift $24.95:
Christmas—Royal Riviera Pears
January—Crisp Mountain Apples
February—Royal Grapefruit

5 box gift $33.95:
January—Crisp Mountain Apples
February—Royal Grapefruit
May—Wild'n Rare Preserves
September—Oregold Peaches

8 box gift $66.95:
Christmas—Royal Riviera Pears
January—Crisp Mountain Apples
February—Royal Grapefruit
May—Wild'n Rare Preserves
August—Exotic Nectarines
September—Oregold Peaches
October—Alphonse LaValle Grapes
November—Royal Beurre Bosc
   Pears

12 box gift $99.95:
Christmas—Royal Riviera Pears
January—Crisp Mountain Apples
February—Royal Grapefruit
March—Royal Oranges
April—Hawaiian Pineapples
May—Wild'n Rare Preserves
June—Home-Canned Fruit
July—Giant Kiwi Berries
August—Exotic Nectarines
September—Oregold Peaches
October—Alphonse LaValle Grapes
November—Royal Beurre Bosc
   Pears

Harry and David

Galaxy

This is a beautifully ribboned tower composed of traditional food favorites in four fancy gift boxes—DeAngelo pears and a crunchy, crisp duo of Delicious apples; 1 lb. in-the-shell mixed nuts—filberts, almonds, walnuts, Brazils, and pecans; a 10-oz. Dobosh Torte; and a 4-oz. box of Danish mints. Available October 15 through December 31.

Assortment above $9.95

Figi's

Indian River Grapefruit

The fabulous Indian River grapefruit—either pink or white—is delicious to eat, wonderful for juicing, and a boon for weight watchers. Included in almost all gift packs, Harvey's will send this versatile fruit alone, shipped fresh from their groves.

⅜ bushel $9.75
½ bushel $10.95
¾ bushel $14.95
1 bushel $17.25

Harvey's Groves

Red Ruby Grapefruit

This is naturally sweet—no sugar needed—Texas red grapefruit. It is fully tree ripened and in season November 15 through April 15.

Single box $9.75
Double-decker $12.95

Figi's

Grapefruit and Avocados

This selection includes famous Fruit-of-the-Month Club grapefruit and Private Label avocados. Six super juicy grapefruit and four hand-selected winter avocados. Available for Christmas delivery only. Supply is limited.

Over 9½ lb. $14.95

Harry and David

Indian River Fruit for Juice

Enjoy the luxury of vitamin-packed, freshly squeezed orange juice, tree ripened and naturally sweetened. Fruit available throughout the season. Pineapple oranges—thin skinned, seedless, easily sliced, versatile—are shipped November through February. You may order all oranges or the combination pack of oranges and grapefruits.

1 bushel $17.95
¾ bushel $14.95
½ bushel $11.75

Harvey's Groves

Kiwi Berries

For the first time this rare, luscious fruit (formerly available only imported from New Zealand) is homegrown. Discover this fantastic *new* fruit with the fabulous strawberrylike flavor. Nine delicious fruits available during November and December.

9-3 or 4 oz. fruits $8.95

The Swiss Colony

Kumquat

This is the Chinese citrus fruit usually cultivated for making preserves and confectionary and available from most Florida shippers. Harvey's adds these delicious morsels to most of their citrus gift baskets. See their catalogue for various ''kumquats-included'' specials.

Harvey's Groves

Persian Limes

An old-time favorite in the tropics for making tall, cool thirst

quenchers—and that very special dessert, lime pie. Florida Persian limes are available from June through August.

¼ bushel $9.95
½ bushel $15.95

R. H. Chamberlin

Mangos

Enjoyed in the Orient before the dawn of recorded history, the mango has been cultivated for over 4,000 years. It has a rich, delicious flavor, a tempting fragrance, and a beautiful color. Florida's choice varieties include the Hayden, Kent, Fascell, Tommy Atkins, Kent, and Keitt.

½ lug $8.95
Full lug $12.95
½ bushel $19.95

R. H. Chamberlin

Olives

The succulent texture and nutlike appearance of the Graber Olive is difficult to describe in words alone. This rare combination of delicious flavor and succulent texture sharpens the appetite. Fresh tinned.

4 7½-oz. tins $6.70
8 tins $11.45
12 tins $15.15

C. C. Graber Co.

Harvey's Oranges

This luscious bargain box contains the choicest oranges—famous Indian River navels, tangelos, or temples (as the seasons dictate) garnished with a special bonus of tangy kumquats. They are delivered grove-fresh to your door.

Approx. 10 lb. Booster Box $6.95

Harvey's Groves

Harvey's Treat of the Month

Season	Variety	Characteristics
December	navel oranges	Christmas delight—medium to large, seedless, mild flavor, easy peeling, excellent in salads for the holidays
January	red tangelos	New Year appetizer—unique combination of orange and grapefruit, deep red color, unusually delightful flavor, seedless, extremely juicy
February	temple oranges	February Charmer—delicate, zipper-skinned, with seeds, sweet tantalizing flavor; medium size
March	honey tangerines	Rare, developed in recent years, likeness of tangerine with the sweetness of honey; sections into bite-size pieces; with seeds
April	pink grapefruit	All-season treat—sweet, seedless, loaded with juice, full of mouth-watering goodness
May	valencia oranges	All-purpose orange—vitamin-enriched, juicy, almost seedless; long lasting, good for eating, slicing for salads, and juicing
3-months (Dec., Jan., Feb.)	⅜ bushel each month	$29.90
	½ bushel each month	$33.50
	¾ bushel each month	$40.35
6-months	⅜ bushel each month	$59.80
	½ bushel each month	$67.00
	1 bushel each month	$102.00

Harvey's Groves

Navel and Temple Oranges

The navels, available November through January, are popular for all uses—peeling, sectioning, slicing, or juicing. These holiday favorites are large, juicy, and seedless. Temple oranges have a short season, January to February 20, but a big demand. This zipper-skinned taste treat is everyone's favorite. Chamberlin will ship individually or in mixed packs. Check with them for current prices.

R. H. Chamberlin

Florida Tempter Oranges

This treat is shipped each month from December through May, and each gift box contains one of the six different Florida orange varieties in season. December, navels; January, tangelos; February, temples; March, Murcotts; April, grapefruit; May, Valencias.

Assortment above $56.95

R. H. Chamberlin

Valencia Oranges

Valencias are available March through May. They are great for fresh fruit salads, fruit cup desserts, and sweet refreshing juice. A springtime treat worth living for!

2/5 bushel $9.95
½ bushel $11.95
¾ bushel $15.95
1 bushel $17.95
1⅓ bushel $23.95

R. H. Chamberlin

Honeyball Comice Pears

These are big, juicy, delicious pears usually not available in stores because only limited quantities of these ''giants'' are grown. Hand-picked and honey-sweet, they are available November 15 to Christmas.

6¾ to 7½ lb. (10 to 14 pears) $7.95

The Swiss Colony

Royal Riviera Pears

Only in Southern France and the Bear Creek Orchards of Oregon has mother nature coaxed pears like these Royal Rivieras to grow. They are a rare treat, so big and juicy that they can be eaten with a spoon. Royal Rivieras are available for delivery between November 10 and January 25 to the connecting 48 states and Hawaii.

Net wt. 6¾ lb. (10–14 large pears) $9.45
Net wt. 9 lb. (23–25 pears) $11.45
Net wt. 7¾ lb. (8–9 1-lb. pears) $11.95

Harry and David

Maverick Royal Riviera Pears

Mavericks they are—fancy they aren't. But they are the same delectable creamy pears as their more photogenic cousins, and still a treat to eat! These mavericks are dappled from too much sun, or burnished where they shouldn't be, or bumped by a limb, or not so very pear shaped, but they are one of the most remarkable bargains in good eating you will ever see.

Order Gift No. 89 (6½ lb.) $8.45
Order Gift No. 88 (20 to 28 pears) $13.95
Order Gift No. 90 (24 lb.) $19.95

Harry and David

Miniature Royal Riviera Pears

These miniatures are just as juicy and flavorful as their big brothers and perfect for a continental dessert tray with cheese, salad, and main-course garnishes. And just plain luscious for out-of-hand eating. Over 9½ pounds of regal feasting.

Order Gift No. 59 $11.45

Harry and David

Honey Tangerines

Murcotts Honey Tangerines are the sweet as honey, easy-to-peel fruit.

They are rapidly becoming one of Florida's most popular hand-eating treats, so enjoy the exquisite flavor.

2/5 bushel $9.95
½ bushel $11.95
¾ bushel $15.95
1 bushel $17.95

R. H. Chamberlin

FRUIT PRESERVES

Apricots and Olives

These imported Apricot preserves with almonds and olives Niçoise with herbs come in two corked-top jars.

1 lb. 5 oz. $15.95

Maison Glass

Candied Fruit

From Italy comes the candied fruit preserved in liquor. Marrons (jumbo chestnuts) in Brandy is also available; price on request from supplier.

Assorted fruit in Brandy 16 oz. $3.50
Cherries in Brandy 9 oz. $4.75
   22 oz. $9.50

English Marmalade

Frank Cooper, Ltd., marmalade manufacturers by appointment to Her Majesty the Queen, offer the following marmalades: marmalade with Cointreau, Oxford marmalade, . vintage marmalade, peel-less orange marmalade.

16-oz. jars $1.95 each

Maison Glass

A French Collection

This one brings you four 12-ounce jars of jam—blue plum, apricot, strawberry and mixed apple, pear, and walnut—beautifully packed and sent along with a box of biscuits.

Assortment $17.95

Maison Glass

Fruits and Berries

These preserves contain no artificial preservatives and no artificial colorings or flavorings—just the pure, natural flavor of the finest Pacific Northwest-grown fruit and berries, quick-cooked in small batches. Package contains five favorites that won the Gold Medal For Excellence at the California State Fair: Wild 'n Rare strawberry, red raspberry, Oregold peach, Wild Mountain blackberry, and wild plum. Packaged in tins, each with its own handy recloseable cover.

5 ¾-lb. tins $9.95

Harry and David

Fruit Cellar

Four sturdy, reusable old-fashioned canning jars come filled with the finest grape jelly, peach butter, strawberry preserves, and apple butter.

4 10-oz. jars $6.95

Figi's

Fruit Spreads

These are full-flavored fruits simmered at low temperature to preserve natural taste. They are less sweet than ordinary preserves. All use natural ingredients, no preservatives. Three jars—one each of strawberry, raspberry, and orange marmalade.

3 10-oz. jars $6.95

Pepperidge Farm

Hawaiian Preserves

Made from fresh Hawaiian fruits and from Hawaiian recipes, these are attractively boxed jars of guava jelly and guava jam, 2 jars of each.

4 7½-oz. jars $6.95 postpaid in U.S.

Kemoo Farm Foods

Jams and Preserves

These are pure jams and jellies made in small batches from high-flavored, specially grown ripe fruit: apple butter (old-fashioned), wild blackberry, black raspberry, rhubarb, blueberry, crabapple butter, peach, peach chop (slow boiled), pear jam, red raspberry, plum jam, spiced blueberry, sour cherry, strawberry (Sparkle), strawberry rhubarb, sweet cherry, tomato ketchup, maple chili sauce.

2 oz. $.80
6 oz. $1.45
9 oz. $1.95

Hickin's

Liqueur Preserves Box

The box contains six jars, one each of: blackcurrant with Rum, peach with Brandy, marmalade with vintage Brandy, marmalade with Scotch whisky, and marmalade with navy Rum.

6 12-oz. jars $17.80

Egertons

Mostarda

These are assorted candied fruits from Italy in clear mustard-flavored syrup that make a sweet spicy relish for boiled or roasted meats or fowl.

1 jar $2.60

Manganaro Foods

Papaya Spread

Papaya is one of the best of all tropical fruits. This spread of papaya is home canned and flavored with honey, pineapple, and lemon. It's a fine food, organically grown, and a delightful spread on bread. It contains no preservatives and should be refrigerated when opened.

1 pt. $2.00
1 qt. $3.00

Ault Bee Farms

Pennsylvania Dutch Preserves

These six jars of the finest Pennsylvania Dutch preserves are chock full of whole large pieces of fruit.

Net wt. 4 lb. 8 oz. $9.50

Great Valley Mills

Preserves, Marmalades, and Jellies

This is a mouth-watering medley: 2¾-ounce jars of strawberry, red raspberry, plum, peach, pineapple and apricot preserves; grapefruit and orange marmalades; crabapple, mint-flavored apple jelly, grape and quince jellies.

Ship wt. 7 lb. $7.75

Figi's

Homemade Strawberry Preserves

Big, ripe strawberries picked at the peak of flavor and cooked at moderate temperatures so not a drop of color or flavor is lost. Uses 25 percent more berries than most recipes. "Fruit-full" goodness is packed into a unique old-fashioned canning jar and sealed tightly.

27 oz. $4.95

The Swiss Colony

Louisiana Strawberry Preserves

These are delectable, whole preserved Louisiana strawberries in an attractive wooden pail.

2½-lb. pail $10.95

Kate Latter's

Wild 'n Rare Preserve Pantry

Here are nine different kinds of homemade Wild 'n Rare preserves and jellies with no artificial flavor or color. There are ¾ pound helpings of each: strawberry preserves, Oregold peach preserves, blueberry preserves, bing cherry preserves, gooseberry preserves, Concord grape jelly, orange marmalade, Bear Creek PearServes, Wild Mountain blackberry preserves.

6¾ lb. $15.95

Harry and David

Fruits in Brandy

Fauchon is considered to be the finest purveyor of choice foods in Paris. Whether fruit, wine, *foie gras,* or a confection, all are divine! To receive a chocolate nougat from Fauchon is likened to receiving a ''gleaming'' nougat from Tiffany! A liter, by the way, equals slightly more than (1.06) a quart.

Fruits à l' Alcool 20° Fauchon (40 proof)	½ liter	1 liter
Abricots (Apricots)	$10.60	$20.40
Ananas (Bananas)	10.85	20.40
Cérises Montmorency (Montmorency cherries)	10.60	18.70
Clémentines (Miniature oranges)	10.75	19.85
Flibustier au Rhum (mixture of fruits)	11.40	20.95
Framboises (Raspberries)	10.40	19.60
Kumquats	10.40	20.65
Marrons	13.70	24.70
Mirabelles à l'Eau de Vie de Mirabelle (Plums in plum liqueur)	10.55	18.50
Oranges en Tranches (Orange slices)	13.35	22.35
Poires Confites, à l'Eau de Vie de Poire (Candied pears in pear liqueur)	12.75	23.25
Pruneaux (French plums)	9.50	15.75
Raisins Muscat (Muscat grapes)	10.60	18.60
Reines-Claudes (Greengages)	10.30	18.50
Vieux Garcon	11.40	20.95

Fauchon

Kate Latter's ESTABLISHED 1928

HONEY

Creamed Honey

A very delicious way to use honey. It is much thicker than clear honey and is especially good spread on bread or toast.

1-lb. jar $2.75, $3.05
2½-lb. jar $4.55, $4.95
(Prices vary according to delivery area.)

Green Mountain Sugar House

English Rose

A Crown Devon jar contains 16 ounces of Fortnum & Mason pure exotic honey.

$8.00. Postage and packing $2.00

Fortnum & Mason

Figi's Honey

Harvested from the hives, this honey comes in six sweet selections: 3 oz. each of Cranmoor (from cranberry blossoms), Sun Flower, Basswood, Buckwheat, Wildflower, and Clover Honey.

18 oz. $5.50

Figi's

Honey Crate

A branded wooden crate is filled with two generous jars of Wild Flower and White Clover honey. The jars are careful reproductions of a honey bottle used in the 1850s.

2 1-lb. jars $4.95

The Swiss Colony

Honey Tea Caddy

Pure honey gathered by the bees of Devon and Cornwall is placed in a Devon pottery container, glazed and decorated with an Old English picture pattern. The lid is fitted with a real seal, making it an ideal kitchen container. Filled with clear or set (thick) honey.

1 lb. $12.00

Egertons

Imported Hungarian Acacia Honey

This is a honey as light and fragile as the flower it is garnered from. It is a shimmering pale golden honey that is not cloyingly sweet but light and crystal clear. Spread it on bread for pure wholesome enjoyment. Use it in baking, as a cereal, or as a dessert topping.

16-oz. jar $2.98
3 jars for $8.00

Paprikas Weiss

Lang Honey

That great, quick-energy food so full of vitamins and minerals and so necessary to good nutrition is available in a choice of Clover, Fallflowers, or Buckwheat.

1 5-lb. pail $6.50
3 5-lb. pails $15.50
6 5-lb. pails $29.00
1 60-lb. pail $51.00

Lang Apiaries

New Zealand Honey

This is White Clover honey from the Canterbury Plains of New Zealand. It is uncooked, organic, and unfiltered. Its exotic flavor is superb.

1-lb. jar $3.50

Calico Kitchens

Thousand Islands Honey

Liquid

3-lb tin Elfin Gold Honey	$ 4.90
Case of 4 3-lb. tins	16.50
6-lb. tin Elfin Gold Honey	8.00
Case of 2 6-lb. tins	15.00

Comb Honey

Case of 24 individually wrapped pieces, each piece 2½ oz. or over	12.00
1 12-oz. piece Comb Honey	2.50
Case of 3 12-oz. pieces Comb Honey	5.00
46-lb. can Liquid Honey	48.00

Creamed Honey (finely granulated)

4½-lb. tin Creamed Honey	6.50
Case of 6 tins	32.50

Thousand Islands Apiaries

Imported Honey

French Honey (Narbonne)	15¾ oz.	$2.90
Mountain Flora (Italy)	12 oz.	2.80
Sicilian Orange Blossom (Mt. Hybla)	1 lb.	2.90

Manganaro Foods

Vermont Honey

This natural product collected by the bees from fragrant Vermont appleblossoms, clover, and wild flowers is available in both light and dark varieties of honey.

8-oz. jar $1.15
1-lb. jar $1.90
2-lb. jar $3.50
5-lb. pail $6.75
1-lb. Honey Bear $1.85
2-lb. Honey Spread $1.90

Harwood Hill Orchard

Vermont Honey Jars

½ lb. $.89
1 lb. $1.49
2 lb. $2.59
5 lb. $5.75

Hickin's

The Mail-Order Food Book

SUGAR

Pearl Sugar

This is the special pearl sugar specified in many continental recipes for candies and desserts. The grains are round and a dull or pearly white, not unlike uncooked tapioca. Best used for decoration only.

17-oz. bag $1.65

Maid of Scandinavia

Maple Sugar

This old-fashioned pure maple sugar is perfect for spooning over desserts or on toast, sandwiches, or pancakes.

1-lb. 14-oz. tin $5.20. Postage and handling $1.50

Sugarbush Farm

Maple Sugar Block

This block of old-fashioned grained sugar is great for all kinds of recipes.

½ lb. $2.90

Green Mountain Sugar House

Maple Sugar Bricks

These pure maple sugar bricks are better for cooking and shaving off pieces rather than for eating, as they are quite hard.

½ lb. $1.75. Postage & handling $1.00

Sugarbush Farm

Soft Maple Sugar

This maple sugar is delicious spread on cereals, toast, everything. And it's useful in recipes too.

1-lb. 14-oz. tin $6.85 or $7.20 depending on delivery area

Green Mountain Sugar House

Dakin Farm
FERRISBURG, VERMONT
05456

MAPLE AND OTHER SYRUPS

Bennington Maple Syrup

A 100 percent pure Vermont syrup, Grade A quality, this is neatly served in a pottery pitcher made in the kiln at Bennington, Vermont.

Pitcher and ½ pt. syrup $8.95
Pitcher and 1 pt. syrup $10.95
Pitcher and 1 qt. syrup $13.95

Pepperidge Farm

Brookside Farm Maple Syrup

Syrup making is akin to wine making in that no two days' production tastes exactly the same. And the syrup made from one grove of maple trees has a different flavor from that made from another grove.

All Vermont maple syrup is made entirely from the sap of maple trees—and it takes about 40 quarts of sap to make *one* quart of syrup. This is the amount of sap that comes from an average maple tree (12 inches in diameter) during the entire sugaring process. The maple-syrup operation of Brookside Farm stores all of the

production in small batches until after the boiling season is over and then selects only complementary flavors to blend as they package the retail containers.

Medium Amber Maple Syrup (Vermont Grade A) is medium amber in color and has a characteristic maple flavor.

Dark Amber Maple Syrup (Vermont Grade B) is dark amber in color and has a heavier, maple-caramel flavor.

Cooking Syrup (Vermont Grade C) is a very dark maple syrup with a pronounced caramel flavor. When used in cooking it imparts a stronger maple flavor than the lighter-colored syrups. This is a good syrup to use when the syrup must compete with an especially strong flavor, such as buckwheat pancakes.

Medium Amber and Medium Dark Syrups: 1 pt. $2.80
2 pt. to one address $5.50
1 qt. $4.25
2 qt. to one address $8.40
1 gal. $13.25
Cooking Syrup: ½ gallon $5.95

Brookside Farm

Dakin Farm Maple Syrup

This is a 100 percent pure Vermont maple syrup. It is available in Fancy Grade or Grade A.

1 pt. $4.10, $4.30, $4.45
1 qt. $6.50, $6.75, $7.00
½ gal. $9.50, $9.95, $10.50
2 ½ gal. $18.00, $19.00, 20.00
(Prices vary according to delivery area.)

Dakin Farm

Embassy Maple Syrup

This gourmet syrup from the snow hills of Vermont is a 100 percent pure New England taste treat. Unsurpassed as a topping for pancakes and waffles, it is available in pints, quarts, and gift packs.

1 pt. $3.70
1 qt. $6.50
5-pack assorted syrups (5 6-oz. cans) $4.50 per pack

Embassy Seafoods

Hickin's Vermont Maple Syrup

This is highest-quality syrup, 100 percent pure, not a blend. Comes in Vermont scenic lithographic cans.

1 gal. $16.95
½ gal. $9.75
1 qt. $6.75
1 pt. $3.95
½ pt. $2.95
2-oz. glass jar $.90

Hickin's

Maine Maple Syrup

A thick, sweet, and natural syrup—100 percent pure—that comes in a handy and attractive jar.

1 pt. $3.50

Especially Maine

Appleyard Maple Syrup

This syrup needs no introduction. A pure maple syrup from Vermont has been a traditional favorite on pancakes or waffles for a long time. And it is being used by more and more cooks in recipes and as an important part of many meals. This syrup is produced without the use of formaldehyde in the tapholes or other chemicals during boiling.

Size	Fancy Grade	Grade A
3 6-oz. cans	N.A.	$4.25–$5.00
1 pt.	$3.25–$ 3.70	3.10– 3.55
1 qt.	5.75– 6.50	5.40– 6.15
½ gal.	9.60– 11.00	8.10– 9.50

(Prices vary according to delivery area.)

The Appleyard Corporation

Green Mountain Maple Syrup

Green Mountain Sugar House operates several maple orchards and trucks all the sap to their central ''sugar house'' for processing. There, three different types of evaporators are used to reduce the sap to syrup. It is started on a very hot oil-fired flue pan to bring it to a quick boil, then passes into the traditional wood-fired evaporator to be nearly finished. As a final stage it passes through a filter tank to partially remove the ''sugar sand,'' then goes into a finishing pan heated by high-pressure steam to bring the syrup to uniform standard. A filter press removes the last of the sugar sand and the syrup goes into the large holding tank from which it is canned hot to ensure keeping quality. Green Mountain Sugar House is the only sugar house in Vermont to use wood, oil, and steam for boiling sap.

Size	Fancy Grade	Grade A	Grade B	Grade C
1 gal.	$13.00	$12.50	$12.00	$8.50
½ gal.	7.50	7.20	7.00	5.10
1 qt.	4.70	4.50	4.30	3.00
1 pt.	2.85	2.75	2.65	N.A.

Green Mountain Sugar House

Harwood Hill Maple Syrup

This is pure Vermont maple syrup; the only additive is Yankee ingenuity. It is available in the usual three grades. Fancy is light amber in color and has a delicately sweet maple flavor; Grade A is medium amber in color and has a sweet maple flavor; and Grade B is dark amber in color and has a richer more caramel flavor.

Size	Fancy Grade	Grade A	Grade B
1 gal.	$16.40	$15.40	$13.40
½ gal.	9.70	8.95	8.40
1 qt.	5.70	5.20	4.55
1 pt.	3.85	3.55	N.A.

Harwood Hill Orchard

Vermont Maple Syrup in Cans

Vermont's greatest contribution to luxury living and luxury giving is this extra-heavy, extra-delicious pure Vermont maple syrup. It can turn breakfasts into real events. It is the answer to that problem gift to suit a whole family—kids and grown-ups.

1 qt. $4.95. $1.60 postage and handling
½ gal. $9.25. $2.50 postage and handling

Sugarbush Farm

Apple Syrup

This is a unique product that is rosy red with just enough taste of the tempting apples from which it is made. Perfect on pancakes, waffles, or ice cream, it comes in an attractively decorated can in a special carton.

½ pt. $1.90
1 pt. $2.75
1 qt. $4.00

Harwood Hill Orchard

Fresh Fruit Syrups

New and delicious, these are made from the best berries and fruits—Wild Blackberry, Black Raspberry (syrup unsweetened, with maple syrup, or sweetened with sugar); Peach, Red Raspberry (syrup unsweetened, with maple syrup, or sweetened with sugar); Strawberry (syrup unsweetened, with maple syrup, or sweetened with sugar); and Apple Syrup.

4 oz. $1.75
6 oz. $2.45
12 oz. $3.65

Hickin's

BUTTERS

Fruit and Nut Butters

	Size	Each	Dozen
Peanut Butter (Eden brand): lightly salted, smooth; made from unblanched dry roasted Virginia peanuts and sea salt	18 oz.	$ .99	$11.88
Cashew Butter (Eden brand): slightly salted	8 oz.	.89	10.68
Peanut Butter (Deaf Smith brand): unsalted, smooth; made from dry roasted organically grown Valencia peanuts	18 oz.	1.10	13.20
Sunflower Butter in Mason jars	1 lb.	1.45	17.40
Sesame Butter: ground from unhulled, toasted sesame seeds with a pinch of salt; in Mason jars	1 lb.	1.40	16.80
Sesame Tahini	1 lb.	1.54	18.48
Apple Butter (Eden butter)	18 oz.	.98	11.76
Apple Butter (Penn Dutch brand) Brother George	18 oz.	1.10	13.20
Apple Sauce (Mrs. Muller's brand): pure apples, unsweetened	1 lb.	.55	6.60
Apple Sauce (Pure and Simple brand)	1 lb.	.50	12.00
Apricot Butter (Pure and Simple brand)	10 oz.	.86	10.32
Cherry Butter	10 oz.	.86	10.32
Grape Butter	10 oz.	.86	10.32
Peach Butter	10 oz.	.86	10.32
Plum Butter	10 oz.	.86	10.32
Raspberry Butter	10 oz.	.95	11.40
Strawberry Butter	10 oz.	.86	10.32

Erewhon

Apple and Plum Butters

Imported Apple Butter 1-lb. can $1.98
Imported Plum Butter 9-oz. jar $.98

Lekvar By The Barrel

Fruit Butters

Selection includes popular Apple Butter and harder-to-find Peach, Apricot, Cranberry, and Orange-Banana butters. Put up in old-fashioned, reusable canning jars.

11-oz. jars $8.95 each

Pepperidge Farm

Macadamia Nut Butter

Here's a butter from Australia that comes packed with a 1-lb. jar of Iron Bark Tree Honey. An exotic taste

treat your senses will not forget. Both honey and butter are guaranteed to be absolutely pure. No salt added.

Gift Box $6.50
Butter only $3.50
Honey only $3.50

Calico Kitchens

10.

BACON

Bacon Packs

These are hickory smoked and savory good. They come packed in cloth bacon bags with suggestions for cooking and using.

2 ¾-lb. packs $8.95

Pepperidge Farm

Swiss Colony Bacon Slab

A choice, lean, whole slab of bacon that is given a mild sweet cure. The bacon is slow-smoked to give it a distinctive flavor. Slice to any thickness you prefer. Cooking

instructions are included.

Net wt. 7–8 lb. $17.95

The Swiss Colony

Todd's Slab Bacon

The unique Old English dry-salt box curing produces a bacon with a surprisingly different flavor that has all its natural goodness heightened by green hickory smoke. Todd's slab bacon is perfect for a less expensive gift or for your own enjoyment. Comes cloth wrapped and beautifully gift packaged.

4–10 lb. per piece $2.19 per lb.

The E. M. Todd Co.

Canadian Style

Braunfels' choice pork loins are lean and tender. They have been carefully cured and slowly smoked over hickory coals the Smokehouse way to produce an unmatched flavor. This bacon is delicious either broiled or baked for breakfast, lunch, or dinner.

3–7 lb. slabs $4.95 per lb.

The New Braunfels Smokehouse

Amana Loin of Canadian Style Bacon

This is the perfect answer for those who can eat no fat. Only the ''eye of the loin'' is selected and specially processed in the slow, Old World tradition. And the old-fashioned smoking captures that wonderful flavor. It comes fully cooked and ready to slice for sandwiches; it may also be fried or roasted.

Net wt. 4–5 lb. $17.95

Amana Society Meat Shop

Canadian-style Loaf

Canadian-style is the finest, most delicate bacon available. This one is very flavorful tender meat formed into a loaf and shipped ready to eat. Each loaf is carefully trimmed to the leanest meat.

1 3/4-2 lb. $11.50

The Swiss Colony

Swiss Colony Canadian

This is a Canadian-style bacon that has been delicately cured and smoked. Comes ready to serve.

2 lb. $9.50

The Swiss Colony

Pepper Bacon

Taste the ''outdoors'' flavor of the specially smoked cut of Pepper Bacon—it's really hearty and robust. Slice as you like it.

1½ lb. minimum $4.95

The Swiss Colony

Side O' Bacon

This is choice, sweet-cured, hickory-smoked Bacon. Slice as you wish.

3¼ lb. minimum $8.95

The Swiss Colony

Sliced Side O' Bacon.

This is the same choice, sweet-cured, hickory-smoked bacon as the regular Side O' Bacon, but it comes sliced for convenience.

2 lb. $5.50

The Swiss Colony

Amber Brand Smithfield Bacon

This is country-flavored slab bacon, the kind you carve yourself. Cured

by the 300-year-old Smithfield process, which includes smoking with woods of oak, hickory, and apple, it comes vacuum-packed in plastic wrap that permanently seals in the southern smokehouse flavor.

3–4 lb. (½ slab) $7.88
6–8 lb. per slab $15.75
8–10 lb. per slab $20.25

The Smithfield Ham and Products Co.

Hickory Smoked Bacon

This old-fashioned slab bacon is bacon as it should be. It has been dry rubbed, sugar cured, and then hickory smoked. Slice it either thick or thin and enjoy its hearty aroma.

Full slab (about 9 lb.) $26.00
½ slab (about 4½ lb.) $14.50
Postage paid in continental U.S.

Ozark Mountain Smoke House

Smoked Country Bacon

Here is the vital ingredient for an old-time hearty breakfast—a robust country bacon. It's dry cured, then gently smoked with hickory.

Completely rindless, so it's easy to slice as thick or thin as you please. Enjoy that mouth-watering hickory aroma as each slice sizzles deliciously in the pan. This is a ''can't miss'' gift for every bacon lover.

4–5 lb. $11.90, $12.40, $12.90, $13.40
7–8 lb. $17.75, $18.35, $18.85, $19.55
2–3 lb. $6.95, $6.95, $7.15, $7.55
(Prices vary according to delivery area.)

Broadbent B&B Food Products

Joyner's Deep Smoked Virginia Bacon

First cousin to the famous Joyner's Smithfield Ham, this bacon is dry cured a minimum of 27 days before being patiently smoked over smoldering hardwood fires. Its rich aroma and hearty old-fashioned flavor are a complement to any meal.

9–11 lb. (average) $2.15 per pound

Joyner Smithfield Hams

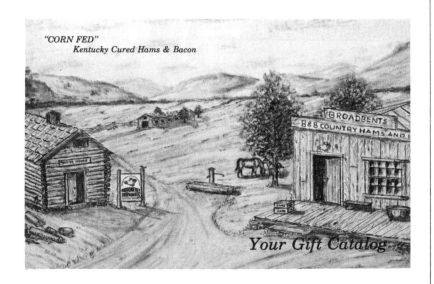

"CORN FED"
Kentucky Cured Hams & Bacon

Your Gift Catalog

Bacon, Pancakes, and Maple Syrup

Enjoy breakfast with buckwheat pancakes, country bacon, and pure maple syrup. This package includes a 2-lb. slab of hickory- and apple-wood-smoked country bacon, ½ pint pure Vermont maple syrup, and a 1-lb. bag of stoneground buckwheat ready-mix.

Net wt. 3 lb. 8 oz. and ½ pt. $9.95

Great Valley Mills

Weaver's Wood Smoked Bacon

This bacon is trimmed from choice, carefully selected corn-fed porkers, then smoked in Weaver's old-fashioned smokehouses. The thick billowy smoke is allowed to penetrate the bacon from both sides, which not only enhances the flavor but also results in less shrinkage per pound when cooked. Weaver's special smoking process produces an

exceptionally rich and smoky flavor you're bound to enjoy. Here is bacon as it should be!

6- to 8-lb. slab (average) $2.50 per lb.
4 1-lb. pkgs. sliced $10.75

Weaver's

Chateaubriand

This regal cut of meat originated in France's great wine-making regions and comes from Omaha boneless and oven-ready. It's the very center cut of the tenderloin, crowned only with enough fat to complement the subtle flavor of the meat. Serves four to six.

4- to 4½ lb. Chateaubriand $44.00

Omaha Steaks International

Corned Beef

Spicy, aromatic seasonings blended with lean, tender beef produce this excellent roll. Serve it traditionally, hot with cabbage, or in delicious hearty sandwiches. Specially selected "eye of the round" cut.

1½–1¾ lb. $7.95

The Swiss Colony

Kosher-style Corned Beef

Omaha's "heirloom blend" of rare spices transforms briskets of the finest corn-fed beef into a zesty treat. This kosher-style brisket is completely free of excess fat. It is fully cooked, ready to heat and eat or serve cold. Shipped October through March.

4- to 4½-lb. brisket $20.50

Omaha Steaks International

Prime Rib Roast

This is prime or choice corn-fed beef at its best. Marbled and meaty, only

the first five ribs are included. And it has just enough fat to enhance its flavor. Easy cooking and serving instructions are included with your order.

12 lb. minimum $59.50

Omaha Steaks International

Heart of Prime Rib Roast

This is a really elegant change-of-pace roast. From prime or choice beef this rib eye roast is memorable whether turned over open coals or oven-roasted. It's boneless and oven-ready and easy to prepare. Cooking and serving instructions are included with your order.

8 lb. minimum $64.50

Omaha Steaks International

Filet Mignon

Demonstrate your "steakmanship" with this showy, boneless center cut from the choicest of beef tenderloins. This steak has been aged to perfection and is so tender that using a knife is more a social gesture than a necessity. Serve these filets simply—piping hot off the grill—or as elegantly as your fancy dictates. A recipe for Bearnaise Sauce by James Beard is included with each order.

Quantity	Weight	Thickness	Price
16	4 oz.	¾"	$41.50
4	6 oz.	1¼"	23.00
6	6 oz.	1¼"	29.00
8	6 oz.	1¼"	35.00
10	6 oz.	1¼"	39.50
16	6 oz.	1¼"	52.00
12	7 oz.	1½"	50.00
10	8 oz.	1¾"	46.00
16	5 oz.	1¾"	46.00
16	5 oz.	1"	47.00
8	9 oz.	1⅞"	46.00
12	9 oz.	1⅞"	60.00
10	10 oz.	2"	54.50
8	12 oz.	2¼"	57.00

Omaha Steaks International

Porterhouse Steaks

For steak lovers who can't decide between a filet and a boneless strip, there's this great alternative—a porterhouse that is a luscious portion of each filet and strip sirloin in a single showy steak. This one is popular with those who love to give—and receive.

Quantity	Weight	Thickness	Price
4	20–22 oz.	1⅛"	$40.00
4	24–26 oz.	1¼"	45.00
2	30–32 oz.	1½"	33.00

Omaha Steaks International

Filets of Prime Rib Roast

Treat yourself to a new world of pleasure. Try this steak cut from the tenderhearted center of a luscious prime rib roast; it has a delicate texture, a luxurious richness, and succulent flavor. Discover this slightly different steak that's equally good at a white tie dinner or at a casual cookout.

Quantity	Weight	Thickness	Price
8	7 oz.	⅞"	$36.50
6	8 oz.	1"	33.00
12	8 oz.	1"	51.00
16	8 oz.	1"	67.50
10	10 oz.	1⅛"	52.50
8	12 oz.	1¼"	52.00

Omaha Steaks International

Boneless Strip Sirloins

This is America's favorite cut—the steak everyone gets excited about. Omaha Steaks' sirloins are naturally aged, beautifully marbled, and trimmed with just enough fat for exceptional flavor. They're delightfully tender, juicy, and tasty.

Quantity	Weight	Thickness	Price
12	7 oz.	¾"	$43.50
10	9 oz.	⅞"	45.50
10	10 oz.	1"	49.00
6	11 oz.	1⅛"	36.50
4	12 oz.	1¼"	31.00
8	12 oz.	1¼"	37.90
12	12 oz.	1¼"	66.00
8	14 oz.	1⅜"	53.50
10	14 oz.	1⅜"	67.00
6	16 oz.	1⅝"	47.90
6	24 oz.	2½"	67.00

Omaha Steaks International

T-Bone Steaks

This item needs no description. Each steak is a truly magnificent ⅞-inch-thick cut of beef. On one side of the bone lies a tender filet; on the other, delectable sirloin. Among the finest beefsteak anywhere.

4 18-oz. steaks $36.00

Omaha Steaks International

Top Sirloins

These are thick and chunky center cuts of the top sirloin, adorned with just a thin crown of fat. Steak lovers appreciate corn-fed flavor and pleasing texture, and Omaha's natural aging makes the difference, imparting a mellow tenderness and enhancing the taste.

Quantity	Weight	Thickness	Price
12	6 oz.	⅞"	$39.00
12	7 oz.	1"	42.50
8	8 oz.	1⅛"	36.00
12	8 oz.	1⅛"	47.50
16	8 oz.	1⅛"	61.75
10	10 oz.	1¼"	48.50

Omaha Steaks International

Omaha Steaks and other gourmet delicacies for you. Enjoy them.

Amana Ham

Amana Boneless Ham—the ''aristocrat of smoked ham.'' This boneless ham is cured in the same old-fashioned way as the regular hams, only all the bone and fat are removed. They are fully cooked and easy to slice. Net wt. 7–8 lb. $27.95

Amana Smoked Ham—cured with a special piquant brine, then hung in a century-old smoke tower until each ham reaches the peak of superb flavor. They are fully cooked, ready-to-eat, and prepared for shipment in sturdy, attractive gift cartons. Net wt. 14–15 lb. $34.95

Amana Society Meat Shop

Boneless Ham

This carefully selected and smoke-cured ham is fully cooked and ready to eat with all of the bone and excess fat removed. It's available September through April.

7¾–8¼ lb. $29.95
3¾–4¼ lb. $16.95

Figi's

Boneless Banquet Ham

This most tender, flavorful deluxe ham is made from specially selected lighter and more tender cuts, with no water or gelatin added. Arrives fully cooked.

7¼ lb. minimum $27.95

The Swiss Colony

Budapest Ham

This boneless cooked ham is tinned and ready to serve. It is very lean and mildly cured with practically no salt to hide its tantalizing flavor.

3-lb. tin $9.98
3 tins $29.00
6 tins $56.00
Original case of 12 tins $109.00

Paprikas Weiss

Country Ham

This is the real thing. It's dry cured with pepper and salt. It's not sugar-cured and not injected with water like ordinary ham. It is salty, but there is no better eating in the world than real country ham.

14 lb. minimum $34.50

Sunnyland Farms

B&B Trigg County Country Ham

This is the specialty of the house! It will fill your kitchen with the indescribable aroma of hickory smoke. Each slice is a delectable morsel of deep ''hammy'' flavor that's a whole world different from other hams. How different? Each one is carefully rubbed with salt, sugar, and other ''secret'' ingredients in precise amounts at certain stages of the curing process. And they are short-trimmed, meaning no long shanks that contain little meat and much extra bone. B&B Country Hams are economical in other ways too. Because of the unique curing and aging process, much more flavor is packed into each bite. Each pound should serve at least six people for dinner as your main course. Whether you prefer your country ham fried or baked, full directions on care, carving instructions, serving suggestions and recipes are included.

Uncooked B&B Kentucky Country Hams—perfect for frying or baking; keep without refrigeration (properly wrapped) for a year:

11–12 lb. $26.75, $27.75, $29.40, $30.00
12–13 lb. $29.05, $30.00, $31.90, $32.90
13–14 lb. $31.30, $32.50, $34.40, $35.50
14–15 lb. $33.60, $34.85, $36.95, $38.10
15–16 lb. $35.90, $37.25, $39.40, $40.70

Cooked Country Hams—table ready; may be frozen; should be sliced very thin; very economical:

7–8 lb. $29.90, $30.60, $31.75, $32.60
8–9 lb. $33.85, $34.60, $35.90, $36.80
9–10 lb. $37.80, $38.60, $40.10, $39.90
10–11 lb. $41.80, $42.70, $44.20, $45.10

(Prices vary according to delivery area.)

Broadbent B&B Food Products

Hermitage Country Ham

Dry salt cured, hand rubbed, and hickory smoked by the original Todd process, this ham has the distinctive flavor and character of Old Virginia Hams. It is ideal for thin slicing and also provides delicious fried ham steaks. Known for generations as a standard of quality unsurpassed in gourmet eating, Todd's hams are uniquely suited for holiday gift giving. They are individually boxed and handsomely gift wrapped.

	per lb.
Hermitage Country Ham:	
12–15 lb. (uncooked)	$2.29
7–11 lb. (fully cooked—bone in)	$3.19
Todd's Old Virginia Ham:	per lb.
13–17 lb. (uncooked)	$2.59
9–13 lb. (fully cooked—bone in)	$3.59
7–9 lb. (fully cooked—boneless)	$4.89

The E.M. Todd Co.

Ozark Mountain Hams

These are all cured the ''Ozark Mountain'' way with a mixture of salt and sugar to give them a hearty flavor without a tough, briny taste. They are smoked with real mountain hickory wood, with a touch of sassafras, and have a real bouncy aroma! Ozark Mountain hams are available uncooked or cooked. There is also a boneless, ready-to-eat ham that has almost no waste.

Uncooked Hams—perfect for frying or baking:

Small uncooked ham	13½–14½ lb.	$36.00
Medium uncooked ham	14½–15½ lb.	38.00
Large uncooked ham	15½–16½ lb.	41.00
Extra-large uncooked ham	16½–17½ lb.	43.00

Fully Cooked Hams—skinned, trimmed, scored, and cloved and then baked slowly in an oven:

Small ready-to-eat ham	10½–11½ lb.	$34.00
Medium ready-to-eat ham	11½–12½ lb.	37.00
Large ready-to-eat ham	12½–13½ lb.	40.00
Extra-large ready-to-eat ham	13½–14½ lb.	43.00

Boneless Ham:

Cured, smoked boneless ham	8½–9½ lb.	$39.00

All prices postpaid in continental U.S.

Ozark Mountain Smoke House

Good hickory smoked Meats

JOYNER'S Smithfield, Va.

JOYNER SMITHFIELD HAMS, BOX 387, SMITHFIELD, VIRGINIA 23430

"CORN FED"
Kentucky Cured Hams & Bacon

Your Gift Catalog

PRICE 35¢

BROADBENT'S B&B PRODUCTS REGISTERED KENTUCKY COUNTRY HAM

CARE OF YOUR B & B COUNTRY HAM

Y YUYGO REGISTERED

COOKED BONELESS SKINLESS **HAM**

SECTIONED AND FORMED WITH NATURAL JUICES - GELATIN ADDED

PRODUCT OF YUGOSLAVIA

INGREDIENTS: FRESH HAM, WATER, SALT, SODIUM PHOSPHATES DEXTROSE, GELATIN, SODIUM NITRITE AND SODIUM NITRATE

NET WEIGHT: 16 OZS. (1 LB.)

EXPORTED BY: "KOPRODUKT" NOVI SAD – YUGOSLAVIA

Omaha Steaks and other gourmet delicacies for you. Enjoy them.

Omaha Steaks International Catalog

1975-76

The Mail-Order Food Book

Peanut City Country Ham

A short-shank ham that has been 100 percent dry cured in salt, smoked very slowly, and carefully aged for from two to three months. It is USDA inspected and comes uncooked. Mild in flavor, this ham does not require soaking or other elaborate preparation. Instructions are included with each ham.

10–12 lb. $19.95 plus shipping charges

The Packing Shed

Ranch Brand Ham

The choicest corn-fed hams are cooked ever so slowly over fragrant embers until tender, juicy, and smoke-sweet, then fully cooked so they can be shipped ready to eat. Available September through April.

9½ lb. minimum $29.95

Figi's

Rather Delightful Ham

Named by an Englishman, this ham is available only as a cooked and ready-to-serve ham. It is larger than most because less moisture is removed; hence it costs considerably less to prepare. Nevertheless, in this day and age it's a superior ham. Rather.

6 lb. $16.40
12 lb. $32.50

McArthur's Smokehouse

Smithfield Ham

These hams are cut from peanut-fed porkers cured by a 300-year-old Smithfield process. Hams are dry salted, spiced, smoked with woods of hickory, apple, and oak and aged from one to two years. Then they are slowly baked, basted in wine, browned, and garnished in the colonial tradition. They come vacuum plastic wrapped, gift boxed, ready to carve, serve, and savor! Smithfield Hams store perfectly and need no refrigeration.

9–10 lb. $39.43
10–11 lb. $43.58
11–12 lb. $47.73

The Smithfield Ham and Products Co.

James River Smithfield Ham

This variety is uncooked and milder flavored than other Smithfield Hams. It is dry salt cured, pepper coated, heavily hickory smoked, and mellowed to perfection by up to six months of aging. Just right to cut into steaks and broil or cut into slices and fry or bake. Wonderful for making ''red eye'' gravy to serve with grits or mashed potatoes. This ham comes uncooked only.

12–14 lb. $32.89
14–16 lb. $37.95

The Smithfield Ham and Products Co.

Joyner's Smithfield Hams

Smithfield Ham production has to move at a leisurely pace. Joyner's hams are still made according to the slow, careful processes that originated back in colonial days. Hardwood for smoking is cut in many of the same groves used more than a century ago. Hams are still carefully moved by hand as many as 89 times during curing and aging. It takes many months, but it produces that sought-after, distinctive flavor of Smithfield Ham.

Joyner's Smithfield Ham—cooked, skinless, fatted, baked and glazed. No additional preparation needed; it is ready to slice and serve. 8–12 lb. (average) $3.25 per lb.

Joyner's Genuine Aged Smithfield Ham—packaged in traditional cloth bags imprinted with easy-to-follow cooking instructions. Costly dry curing, unhurried smoking over fragrant hardwood fires, and months of patient aging combine to concentrate distinctive, rich flavor in every morsel. 11–17 lb. (average) $2.35 per lb.

Joyner's Red Eye, Red Gravy Ham—one of the classics of southern cooking. These hams are plump, meaty, and closely trimmed. They are processed to exacting standards that assure country-style goodness every time. Red Eye Hams are pepper coated, carefully aged, baked, and glazed—ready to slice and serve. 10–16 lb. (average) $2.05 per lb.

Joyner Smithfield Hams

Smoked "Hunky Dory" Ham

Lean, tender, 10- to 13-pound prime whole hams with the most persnickity pedigrees ever! Evenly sugar-cured the hard way—by hand—then smoked to rosy perfection. They are fully cooked and ready to serve. Or heat them for a couple of hours, then glaze them with Harry's gourmet glaze (recipe included).

Order Gift No. 381 $39.95

Harry and David

McArthur's Smoked Ham

Old Fashioned Smoked Ham—chock full of real early-American flavor. An eating ham, not just for nibbling. McArthur hams are bathed in molasses for 7 weeks, soaked in fresh water for 24 hours to remove excess salt, and then soaked for 3 days over sap-filled hickory logs. Needs no boiling or soaking.
6 lb. (average) $18.25
12 lb. (average) $36.50
Fully Baked Smoked Ham—the same ham as above but already baked and glazed in the McArthur ovens just as you would bake it at home. It is ready

to slice and serve; if you prefer, bake an hour to warm.

5 lb. (average) $19.75
10 lb. (average) $39.50
Fully Baked Boneless Ham—cured just as it was 100 years ago, with an old-fashioned process that includes no pumps or needles, or fast cures or shortcuts. 4¾ lb. (average) $24.00
Ham Morsels—come in eight-ounce packages. 1½ lb. $7.95

McArthur's Smokehouse

Pennsylvania Dutch Smoked Ham

Delicious Pennsylvania Dutch old-fashioned cured and triple-smoked hams are chosen from the choicest corn-fed hogs. They are prepared by the old method, trimming away unnecessary outside fat so that spiced vinegar and sugar will penetrate deep into the meat while laying in cure for many weeks, then slowly smoked for two weeks over apple and hickory wood.

10–12 lb. $27.50
14 lb. 32.50
16 lb. 35.00

Great Valley Mills

Pepperidge Farm Smoked Ham

Already baked and ready to eat, this ham was selected for its tenderness and flavor and lazily smoked in the old-fashioned way—pungent hickory smoke. Satisfaction guaranteed.

½ Ham 6 lb. $23.50
Whole Ham 12 lb. $39.95

Pepperidge Farm

Weaver's Famous Wood Smoked Ham

The tempting flavor of Weaver's ham is the direct result of prime selection and longer, deeper smoking over

specially aged hardwood in their old-fashioned smokehouses. Their special smoking process produces a ''dryer'' ham, with less shrinkage and a greater edible yield per pound than commercially produced ham. The tempting flavor and downright good taste of Weaver's deep-smoked ham is a taste treat that makes any

meal a festive occasion. And it makes mouth-watering snacks and sandwiches.

10–14 lb. (average) $2.75 per lb.

Weaver's

Country-style Ham Steaks

These are tender, juicy center slices dry-cured the southern country way. Each ham is hand rubbed to control salt, and the secret dry-curing formula ensures a texture and taste that you won't believe.

6 6-oz. steaks $17.50
12 6-oz. steaks $32.00
6 8-oz. steaks $19.95
12 8-oz. steaks $37.00

Omaha Steaks International

Boneless Leg of Spring Lamb

Here's a succulent delicacy. This delightfully sweet and tender meat is oven-ready. The bone has been removed and the leg tied for roasting. A new recipe by James Beard is enclosed with your order.

6½–7½ lb. $40.50

Omaha Steaks International

Spring Lamb Chops

Delight the most fastidious with these choice, tender spring lamb center-cut chops. They are fine grained and the flavor is unusually sweet.

10 6-oz. French rib chops 1¼″ thick $36.50
12 6-oz. loin chops (tenderloins left in) 1⅜″ thick $38.00

Omaha Steaks International

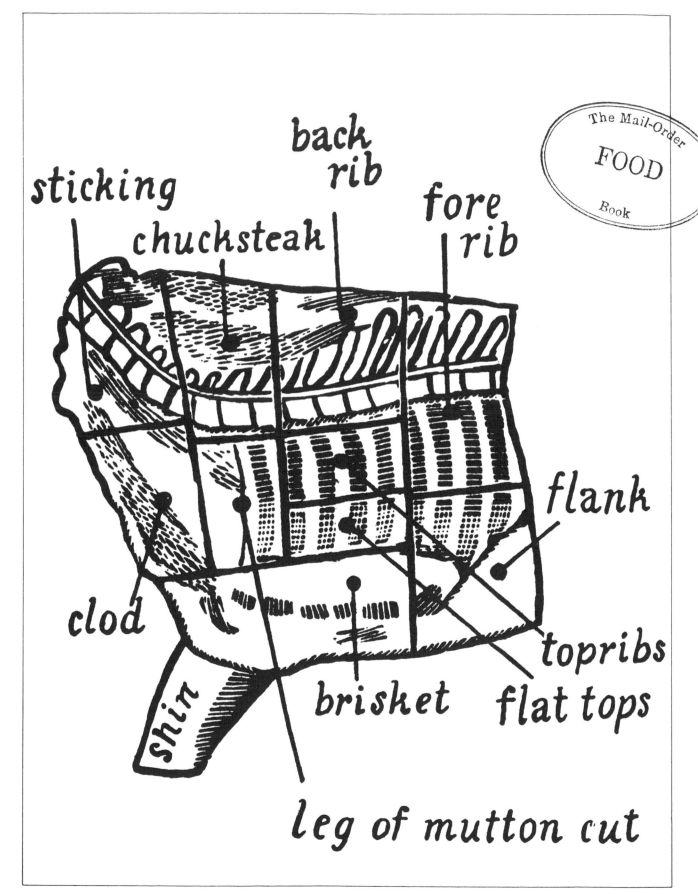

sticking

chucksteak

back
rib

fore
rib

The Mail-Order
FOOD
Book

flank

clod

shin

brisket

topribs

flat tops

leg of mutton cut

PORK

Sugar Cured Smoked Pork Loin

Eat ''high on the hog'' with this almost fat-free boneless smoked loin. It may be sliced thin and served cold or fried lightly for breakfast or supper. It is perfect for Eggs Benedict. The loin, which weighs about five pounds, is cut into three pieces, and each piece is vacuum packed.

About 5 lb. $23.00 postage paid in continental U.S.

Ozark Mountain Smoke House

Smoked Pork Shoulder

Delicious, succulent meat, lightly smoked and truly sweet, smoked carefully with hickory, this lean, boneless pork cut is ready to eat or can be baked, boiled, or fried to bring out its juicy flavor. A sweet morsel.

1½ lb. minimum $7.50

The Swiss Colony

Pork Tenderloin Filets

These boneless center cuts from the tenderloin are everything you would expect from pork ''filet mignon.'' Bake, fry, or broil them, you'll remember their goodness for a long time. A recipe for Pork Tenderloin Chinese is enclosed with your order.

12 4-oz. filets $24.50
24 4-oz. filets $36.50

Omaha Steaks International

Paprikas Hungarian Brand Sausage

This sausage is made by Hungarian specialists according to a time-tested recipe using only pure pork and sweet Hungarian paprika. It is cured for months to give it a very mild, smoky flavor.

1 lb. $4.95
5 lb. $24.00
10 lb. $46.00

Paprikas Weiss

SAUSAGE

B&B Sausage

B&B Sausage Assortment—combines an old favorite—beef and pork summer sausage—with three new sausages that are sure to please every sausage fancier. The assortment contains a 14-ounce roll of B&B Summer Sausage and 12-ounce rolls each of hearty All Beef Summer Sausage, zesty Beer Sausage, and particularly delicious Black Knight Summer Sausage. This assortment is available November through April. $9.65–$10.60 depending on delivery area. *Summer Sausage*—beef and pork summer sausage zesty and full bodied with just the right mixture of spices. B&B Summer Sausage needs no refrigeration, but keep an extra in your freezer. $5.85–$6.50 depending on delivery area.

Broadbent B&B Food Products

Sausage Assortment

Assortment includes 6 ounces each of All-Beef Summer Sausage, tasty Braunschweiger, tangy Pizza Sausage, and Beerwurst. It's available September through April.

Ship wt. 3 lb. $6.50

Figi's

Double-smoked Sausage

Top-quality spices and meats, and generations of experience, make these double-smoked sausages. The ''Smoked Sausage'' pack contains All Beef Summer Sausage, Braunschweiger, Metwurst, Pizza Sausage, Beerwurst, and extra-lean Black Jack Summer Sausage—a total of 3¾ pounds.

Ship wt. 6 lb. $11.95

Figi's

Long, Long Sausage

Here's 10 feet of sausage—zesty all-beef sausage.

Net wt. 1½ lb. $7.95

The Swiss Colony

Amana Summer Sausage

The selection of only the finest ingredients, a blend of rare imported spices, and over 100 years of know-how in the art of meat smoking is the basic formula that makes these ''twins'' (light-smoked and double-smoked Summer Sausage) a favorite of all who taste them.

Sausage Twin Pack Net wt. 2 lb. $7.50

Amana Society Meat Shop

Hickory Smoked Summer Sausage

Although called summer sausage, this is a perfect year-round snack. It is made from a blend of beef, pork, and spices first stuffed into a two-inch casing and then hickory smoked and fully cooked. Each stick weighs about 2 pounds and is about 2 feet long.

1 stick $9.00 postage paid in continental U.S.

Ozark Mountain Smoke House

Three-Foot Sausage

Here's a giant sausage using only the finest beef (no pork) laced with unusual spices in a superb recipe. It's specially cured, expertly smoked, and air-dried. Keeps fresh or frozen.

Net wt. 4 lb. $13.95

The Swiss Colony

VEAL

Veal Cutlets

Young milk-fed vealers produce these tender, scrumptious cuts that have only a hint of fat. Slow cooking keeps them tender and brings out their best flavor. A recipe is enclosed with your order.

18 4-oz. cutlets ⅜" thick $47.50

Omaha Steaks International

Veal Saddle Roast

This delicate boneless veal roast has been expertly trimmed from the finest milk-fed calves. The special milk feeding (developed by the Dutch)

Sausage Patties

Generous patties of pure pork are combined with selected seasonings and spices that make for a sausage worth talking about—and eating. Sizzling hot, their tantalizing aroma will bring family and guests clamoring to your table.

18 2-oz. portions $18.50
45 2-oz. portions $22.50

Omaha Steaks International

gives this veal its firm, lean texture and creamy white color.

2½ lb. minimum $31.50

Omaha Steaks International

Veal T-Bone Steaks

These petite servings, sizzling hot, have a flavor few people can resist. Cut from finely grained, pink, and velvety meat from choice milk-fed dairy calves, they are a dining sensation.

18 5-oz. steaks ⅝" thick $37.50

Omaha Steaks International

CURED AND SMOKED MEATS

meats. In 1885 Daniel Weaver made the first Lebanon bologna commercially and created the famous Weaver's recipe. This recipe is a carefully guarded family secret handed down to each generation. Practically all the Lebanon bologna consumed in the United States is processed in the Lebanon Valley. It is considered a gourmet food and is enjoyed throughout the world.

1½ lb. roll $5.95
3½ lb. roll $10.50
8- to 9-lb. roll $2.50 per lb.

Weaver's

Dried Beef

Like all their other products, Weaver's famous wood-smoked dried beef is processed according to a carefully guarded family secret. Their old-fashioned smokehouses give their meat its distinctive original flavor. This dried beef is a flavorful treat that is hard to beat.

4- to 6-lb. piece $3.95 per lb.
4 1-lb. pkgs. sliced $17.95

Weaver's

Beef Log

This log is made from the finest beef (no pork). The highest-quality meat and delicate herbs and spices are blended and cured in a very special way. Each Beef Log is carefully smoked over real hickory embers, then air-dried.

Net wt. 2 lb. $5.95

The Swiss Colony

Boar

Imported from Poland, tinned and ready to heat and serve, here is roast wild Boar in juniper sauce.

14¾-oz. tin $4.98
3 tins for $14.00
6 tins for $27.00

Paprikas Weiss

Weaver's Famous Lebanon Bologna

This bologna is hung in the thick billowy smoke produced by aged hardwoods in Weaver's old-fashioned smokehouses and is prized by gourmets for its tangy, spicy flavor and authentic smokehouse aroma. It is one of the world's unique foods—sensational as an hors d'oeuvre, snack brunch, or luncheon treat.

In the early 1880s the Pennsylvania Dutch settlers in Lebanon, Pennsylvania, began making the sausagelike food known today as Lebanon bologna. Many families developed their own recipes and took delight in mixing unusual combinations of herbs, spices, and

Lebanon, Beer, and Ring Bologna

Here's a combination of pure beef Lebanon bologna, old-fashioned beer bologna, and a ring bologna that are government inspected and made from the finest meats and spices.

Net wt. 2 lb. 10 oz. $8.50

Great Valley Mills

Ham and Bacon

A ten-pound ham, Pennsylvania Dutch and triple smoked, that can be eated as received or heated in your oven. The recipe is included with every ham. And four pounds of slab bacon, cured in the same manner as the ham.

Net wt. 14 lb. $37.50

Great Valley Mills

Jerky

Pemmican brand hickory-smoked buffalo jerky brings the flavor of the old West into your kitchen with a hickory-smoked taste treat. These nuggets are made from lean buffalo meat, the food staple of the early American Indians and frontiersmen. Bite-sized tidbits that add new zest and flavor to favorite foods have been coarsely ground in a blender and can be used in place of bacon for garnishing. Ground into flakes and sprinkled into batter, they add a new dimension to pancakes, waffles, and breads.

Pemmican jerky is made from buffalo raised commercially, just like beef cattle, on a 60,000-acre ranch near Gillette, Wyoming, separate and apart from the herd of buffalo protected by the National Park system. All meat is processed at a federally inspected plant, smoked with real hickory wood, and vacuum packed to retain freshness for six months.

¾-oz. $1.25 plus $.25 postage
2 packages for $2.50 total

Sourdough Jack's

Liverwurst

A full, rich flavor and unusual creamy texture distinguish this handsome sausage from any other liver sausage. Spreads like butter.

Net wt. 2 lb. $5.50

The Swiss Colony

Pastrami

Specially selected from the lean and tender "eye of the round," this richly peppercorned and spiced pastrami roll just melts into hot sandwiches.

1½ lb. minimum $8.95

The Swiss Colony

Salami

A combination of beef and pork salami where just the right amount of beef has been added to the salami to give it the full-bodied taste of rich, red-blooded meat. The seasoning has been toned down, but it's still zesty,

with a delicate, subtle pungency.

1, 2, 3, or 6 lb. $3.98 per lb.

Paprikas Weiss

Hard Salami

This is a special Swedish favorite—a hearty sausage, much prized for its light, smoky flavor and mellow taste. Pork meat only is chopped moderately fine and then blended with distinctive seasonings. Sausage, free of garlic and perfect for parties or lunches. And it keeps well.

1½ lb. minimum $6.95

The Swiss Colony

Soft Salami

Here's a sensational smoky, spicy salami made from tender, lean beef and specially selected pork cuts and touched with a hint of garlic, imported seasonings, and spices.

Net wt. 2 lb. $6.95

The Swiss Colony

Scrapple

Packed in a useful basket come one tin of the finest country scrapple, one pound bag of stoneground buckwheat ready-mix, and a jar of real Pennsylvania Dutch apple butter cooked slowly over wood fires.

Net wt. 3 lb. 3 oz. $6.95

Great Valley Mills

Scrapple and Bacon

Contains three one-pound cans of scrapple and approximately two pounds of sliced bacon. Oven-broil the triple-smoked bacon and pan-fry the scrapple. The scrapple is so lean that butter has to be added when cooking.

Assortment $11.95

Great Valley Mills

Venison

Here's a variety of Polish game products tinned and ready to serve: Venison with Mushrooms, Venison with Chanterelle Mushrooms, Venison Deer Filets, Deer Goulash with Mushrooms. Order just one, or a selection.

14¾-oz. tin $4.98
3 tins for $14.00
6 tins for $27.00
30-oz. tin Deer Goulash with Chanterelles $6.95

Paprikas Weiss

Amana Variety Packages

Sausage and Bacon—a triple treat! A slab of bacon with that truly distinctive smoky flavor, and one each of the Famous Twins, double-smoked summer sausage and light-smoked summer sausage. Net wt. 3 lb. $8.95

V.I.P. Special—a gift of distinction! Ideal for hors d'oeuvres, snacking, and anytime eating. Contains chunk of Canadian bacon, double-smoked summer sausage, sliced smoked bacon, Swiss cheese, Cheddar cheese, horseradish, light-smoked summer sausage. Net wt. 7–8 lb. $19.95

Dutch Lunch Kit—a ready-to-eat assortment for a "Dutch treat" or treat anytime! Contains a light-smoked summer sausage, double-smoked summer sausage, Swiss cheese, Cheddar cheese, horseradish. Net wt. 4 lb. $11.95

Amana Society Meat Shop

The Mail-Order Food Book

Weaver's Variety Packages

Gift Package—a variety of good old-fashioned Pennsylvania Dutch delicacies. There's something in this assortment to enrich every meal. Contains 3½-lb. pure beef roll Lebanon bologna, 1 lb. wood-smoked dried beef, 1-lb. package sliced wood-smoked bacon. $18.50

Variety Box—a tantalizing assortment to bring smiles of delight from the most critical of gourmets. Contains 1-lb. package sliced Lebanon bologna, 1-lb. package sliced sweet bologna, 1-lb. package sliced wood-smoked bacon, 1-lb. package sliced wood-smoked dried beef. $13.95

Bell Ringer—a box full of Pennsylvania Dutch treats for breakfast to dinner. Contains a 2-lb. piece of Canadian bacon, a 1-lb. package of wood-smoked beef, 1½ lb. smoked pure beef roll Lebanon bologna. $19.95

Deluxe Sampler—a delectable assortment of smoked-meat products. There's a taste treat for every member of the family in this generous package, including 1 lb. each of sliced Lebanon bologna, sweet bologna, wood-smoked bacon, beef and pork sausage, wood-smoked dried beef, and a 2-lb. piece of Canadian bacon. $24.95

The Big Three—a winning combination of Pennsylvania Dutch taste treats that will delight all who enjoy good food. Contains a 10- to 14-lb. wood-smoked ham, a 1-lb. package of wood-smoked bacon, and a 1½-lb. roll of pure beef Lebanon bologna. $39.95

Weaver's

11.

Almonds

Hickory-smoked almonds that are crisp and crunchy and zippy tasting! These are really delicious before dinner or with cocktails. These big California almonds have that good old hickory-smoked flavor plus a distinctive peppery tang.

2-lb. 4-oz. Gift Box $7.65
3-lb. Home Box $9.15

Sunnyland Farms

Slivered Almonds

These are a real hit with good cooks! They are top-quality blanched nonpareils, cut to just the right size. They are ready for use in vegetables, salads, and fish dishes or in your favorite cake recipe.

3-lb. Home Box $8.80
Case of 6 shipped to one address $44.00

Sunnyland Farms

Imported Chestnut Stuffing

A ready-to-use blend of chestnuts, toasted bread, milk, and spices.

16-oz. tin $2.98
3 tins $8.00
6 tins $15.00

Paprikas Weiss

Macadamia Nut Tower

Includes Hawaiian macadamia nuts combined in three delicious ways: 8 ounces (2 layers) of the finest macadamia chocolates, 10 ounces of macadamia brittle, and 10 ounces of macadamia nuts in colorful tins.

Assortment above $10.95

The Swiss Colony

Roasted Peanuts

These are farm-fresh Georgia Goobers. They have been roasted in a carefully controlled heat for just the right length of time. Deee-licious!

2-lb. tin $4.95
6-lb. Home Box $7.50
Case of 4 2-lb. tins shipped to one
address $14.50

Sunnyland Farms

Georgia Runner Peanuts

A flavorful source of protein, these
large peanuts are super. Roast them,
make your own peanut butter, or put
them in all kinds of casseroles. A
recipe is enclosed with each
shipment.

1–9 1½-lb. bags $1.55 per bag
10–23 1½-lb. bags $1.40 per bag
1–4 cases $32.50 per case
24 bags per case
6-lb. box $5.75

Koinonia Products

Home-cooked Salted Peanuts

Here's a traditional Tidewater
Virginia delicacy. Selected Virginia
Jumbos are salted but free of
additives, vegetable gum, starch, or
other preservatives. Their perishable
nature requires refrigeration. These
peanuts are shelled, water-blanched,
cooked in oil, salted, and packed in
tins.

2 lb. 14 oz. $5.95 plus shipping
charges
1 lb. 4 oz. $3.50 plus shipping
charges

The Packing Shed

Salty Peanuts

A new flavor to delight tastebuds,
these peanuts are soaked in a
salt-sugar-vinegar-water solution for
a few minutes, dried, then popped
into a large oven and dry-roasted for
that special tangy taste.

1–9 1½-lb. bags $1.95 per bag
10–23 1½-lb. bags $1.90 per bag
1–4 cases $42.00 per case
1–29 10-oz. boxes $1.10 per box

1–4 cases $30.00 per case
1–11 2-lb. tins $3.95 per tin
1–4 cases $37.80 per case
24 bags per case

Koinonia Products

South Georgia Peanuts

South Georgia farmers grow
America's most delicious peanuts.
Sunnyland buys them from a sheller
in Dawson, Georgia, then regrades
and hand-picks them so you get only
the finest. They come from a new
crop and are freshly shelled so you
get them at the peak of their flavor.
Each box includes a Peanut Fact
Folder with storage instructions and
recipes.

4⅜-lb. box $5.25
8-lb. box $7.60
Case of 6 4-lb. boxes shipped to one
address $25.00

Sunnyland Farms

Spiced Peanuts

Try these specially spiced delights
made in the same way as the
Koinonia spiced pecans—with gobs
of large peanuts treated in the same
spicy way bringing out both the
peanut and cinnamon flavors.

1–29 9-oz. boxes $.95 per box
1–4 cases $24.00 per case
1–9 1-lb. bags $1.30 per bag
10–23 1-lb. bags $2.25 per bag
1–4 cases $25.20 per case
24 bags per case

Koinonia Products

Fancy Shelled Pecans

Direct from the growing area, this is
pecan meat that is the sole survivor of
a most exacting process of
selection—rigid standards for flavor,
richness, size, oil content, color, and
shape. Enjoyed by discriminating
people around the world, they are
delicious as they are or roasted.

Perfect for baking, candy, or salads,
these premium-quality pecans make
great gifts.

2 lb. $7.50
3 lb. $10.75
5 lb. $16.50
10 lb. $30.00

Sternberg Pecan Company

Hickory Smoked Pecans

The superb robust flavor of fresh,
plump pecan halves combined with
old-fashioned hickory smoke is a
gourmet's delight. Packaged
attractively, this makes a stunning
gift.

Net wt. 9 oz. $6.65
Net wt. 1½ lb. $12.45

Priester's Pecans

Koinonia Pecans

In the shell, shelled, halves, pieces,
hickory smoked—all are a
mouth-watering delight.

Hickory-smoked pecans—made crisp
and tantalizing by slow smoking for
14 hours over a low hickory fire, then
sprinkled with a little salt and butter.
Write for current prices.

Pecans in the Shell—Georgia's finest
plump, carefully hand-selected
pecans of top variety. Large,
good-looking pecans in their natural
unpolished color. Keep a bowl full
handy where you like to sit and talk.
The ''work'' of shelling your own
makes them even more enjoyable.
5-lb. box $7.65
8½-lb. box $12.65
28-lb. box $37.00

Shelled Pecan Halves—large,
flavorful, freshly shelled from the
choicest tree-ripened pecans. Just the
right balance of the delicate oils that
make pecans so good to eat.
1–9 1-lb. bags $3.25 per bag.
10–23 bags $2.95 per bag.

1–29 7-oz. boxes $1.70 per box.
1–4 cases $45.00 per case.
1–11 1-lb. 8-oz. tins $6.10 per tin.
1–4 cases $63.00 per case.

Spiced Pecans—nice big pecans,
coated with sugar, cinnamon, and
butter. A delicious spicy taste that
blends really well with top-quality
pecans. An unusual combination.
Write for current prices.

Koinonia Products

Roas'tin Pecans

Roas'tins are fancy mammoth-size
pecan halves freshly roasted to
perfect crispness and lightly
sprinkled with finely ground salt.
These pecan halves are specially
selected for their good roasting
qualities. After roasting, they're
immediately packaged and sealed,
which keeps the contents
roaster-fresh. Comes in a beautiful
imported tin from England.

Net weight 2 lb. $9.35
Case of 12 shipped to one address
$105.20

Priester's Pecans

Schleys Pecans

Schleys are the most delicious pecans
grown. Although smaller than other
varieties, their very thin shells are
easily cracked in your hand, and their
unusually firm-textured meats, which
are high in polyunsaturated oils, give
them an unusual flavor. Schleys are
difficult to grow, so their production
is limited.

5-lb. Gift Box $8.55
10-lb. Gift Box $15.00
25-lb. Gift Box $37.00
Case of 5 5-lb. Gift Boxes shipped to
one address $37.50

Sunnyland Farms

Stuart Pecans

Stuart Pecans—big, bright, firm,
tasty meats—are the nuts that built
Georgia's pecan industry. Bigger
than Schleys (they're about 1 inch in
diameter), their shell is a bit thicker,
thus they keep longer. They are still
easy to crack, either by hand or with
a nutcracker.

5-lb. box $7.85
9-lb. box $12.95
25-lb. box $33.50

Sunnyland Farms

Joe Williams Pecans

Freshly shelled and freshly packed,
these whole halves solve your
gift-giving problems. These shelled
pecan meats are selected and packed
from the largest and best nuts
available.

1 container $9.50
2 containers $9.40 each
6 or more containers $9.30 each

2 lb. containers.

Joe Williams

Pecans: Natural Mammoth Halves

Pecans that have been meticulously
selected for their size, quality, and
flavorfulness, these rich and meaty
pecans are packaged in an intricately
designed imported tin.

Net weight 2 lb. $8.95
Case of 12 shipped to one address
$99.50

Priester's Pecans

Pecans: Selected Whole Halves

These are selected meats from the
largest and best nuts available,
freshly shelled and freshly packed!

They make a pleasing and different
gift for any occasion.

Net wt. 3 lb. per container
1 container $9.50
2 containers $9.40 each
6 or more containers $9.30 each

Joe Williams

Bag-O-Pistachios

A rustic burlap bag holds a full
measure—2½ pounds—of colossal
size, easy-to-open natural and
colored pistachios.

Ship wt. 3 lb. $10.95

Figi's

California Pistachio Nuts

These California pistachios are larger
than the imported Colossals. They
are natural—no dye is used.

1½-lb. Gift Tin $8.50
2-lb. bulk pack $8.00

Calico Kitchens

Iranian Pistachios

Roasted and salted in the shell, pistachios make some of the finest nibbling imaginable. They are growing in popularity faster than any other nut. Like pecans, pistachios can vary widely in quality and flavor. Sunnyland is lucky in having a good supply of the famous Iranian Colossals.

Net wt. 1 lb. 12 oz. (Gift Tin) $8.00
Net wt. 3 lb. (Home Box) $10.85
Case of 9 Gift Tins shipped to one address $60.00
Case of 4 Gift Tins shipped to one address $28.00

Sunnyland Farms

Shah of Iran Pistachio Nuts

Grown in Iran, they are harvested at the peak of maturity, hand picked, specially roasted, and salted by a unique process, then vacuum packed.

2 12-oz. tins $10.95

C. C. Graber Co.

Supreme Quality Pistachios

These are available for the first time in the United States. They are natural, lightly salted, and bursting from their shells.

1 lb. $6.50

Plumbridge

Black Walnuts

Fancy large-size black walnut pieces from the Ozark Mountain country (should not be confused with English walnuts, which are much more bland), their pungent aroma adds zest to most recipes that call for nuts. They are grand for dessert toppings, cakes, and puddings and also when sprinkled on salads.

3-lb. 13-oz. box $10.15
5-lb. box $16.30

Sunnyland Farms

English Walnuts

Gourmet chefs use English walnuts almost as much as they do pecans. Sunnyland brings you the best light California walnut pieces. They are freshly shelled from quality new-crop nuts and shipped at the peak of their flavor. An English Walnut Fact Folder and recipes are included in each box.

3½-lb. box $8.60
9-lb. box $19.50
Case of 5 3½-lb. boxes shipped to one address $39.75

Sunnyland Farms

Assorted Nuts

Included are mammoth pecans, cashews and almonds, fancy Brazils, choice pistachios, and macadamias. Roasting in small batches brings out their delicate flavors.

Net wt. 2 lb. $8.95

The Swiss Colony

Mixed Nuts

A Bear Creek Canoe features six different kinds of roasted nuts: premium Oregon filberts, jumbo pistachios, imported cashews, extra large southern pecans, barbecue flavor whole almonds, and Hawaiian macadamias. Each is roasted to the peak of perfection, lightly salted, and beautifully gift packaged in six recloseable tins, and vacuum packed for best keeping quality. Over 1¼ pounds.

Order Gift No. 368 $12.95 delivered

Harry and David

Totem Nuts

Here's the newest, tastiest thing that has happened to a nut—peanuts, filberts, pistachios, almonds, cashews, Brazils, and macadamias—one or all. The nuts are dry roasted and crisp coated in a unique process discovered in Mexico and patented in the United States. Try these different taste treats with the fresh, snappy flavor. Write supplier for details, prices—and a sample.

Kakawateez

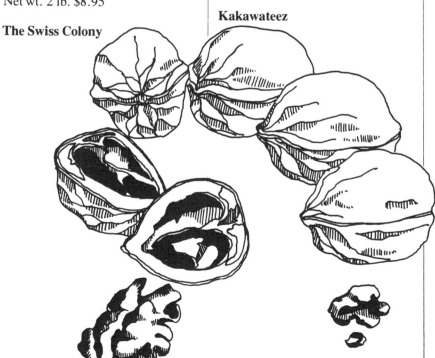

12.

ORGANIC FOODS

The "organic" movement has taken hold not only in the United States but in Europe and other parts of the world as well. People everywhere have begun to worry about the pesticides and chemicals in their food and about carcinogenic hormone products that have been found in meat. And they have also discovered that organic food tastes better.

The term "organic" or "organically grown" implies that plants or trees have been cultivated by natural methods, thereby excluding chemical fertilizers, insecticides, and fumigants. "Naturally grown" should be interpreted to mean that trees or plants have grown without human intervention and without being subjected to chemicals or sprays.

Beans and Grain

Walnut Acres, in Penns Creek, Pennsylvania, has been called "an overgrown home kitchen producing handcrafted natural foods." They are one of the oldest and best-known producers of natural, organic foods, having raised organic foods for over 30 years. They have never used synthetics, preservatives, or the like. Walnut Acres, a rambling farm of about 500 acres, is devoted mainly to the cultivation of grains and

seeds—alfalfa, whole wheat, rye. In addition, the farm works these grains and seeds into a variety of semifinished products—barley, corn meal, gluten flour, muffin meal, rye cereal, wheat germ. And they cultivate many kinds of vegetables—kidney beans, lentils, peas, corn, tomatoes, pumpkin, beets.

Walnut Acres also prepares fruit juices, soups, peanut butters, canned fruits, and vegetables.

Grains and Beans:

Azuki beans	3 lb.	$4.64	(1 lb. $1.59)
Barley	3 lb.	1.62	(1 lb. $.58)
Buckwheat groats (whole, hulled, raw)	3 lb.	2.85	(1 lb. $.64)

Walnut Acres

Deer Valley Bakery Bread

Carsten's Deer Valley Farm has been devoted to organic farming since 1947. All their organic products are guaranteed organically grown without chemical fertilizers or poisonous sprays; organic items not produced at Deer Valley must meet their standards. Natural items are carefully selected.

Deer Valley Bakery specializes in baking 100 percent organically grown whole grain breads, cookies, and cakes. All the whole grain flour and raw milk and eggs used at the bakery comes from the farm. Other ingredients, such as dried fruit, honey and nuts, and maple syrup, are also organic. Only natural oils and fats are used in baking and cooking. Deer Valley yeast-raised breads and pastries are sweetened with honey, maple syrup, and unsulphured molasses only.

In addition to its breads and pastries, Deer Valley carries grains, seeds, nuts, flours, and herb teas.

Whole Grain Bread

Cornell Formula Bread (natural unbleached flour)	1 lb. 2 oz.	$.65
Cornell Rye, 50% Cornell, 50% Rye	1 lb. 2 oz.	.65
Italian Cornell	1 lb. 2 oz.	.70
Whole Grain Raisin Bread	1 lb. 4 oz.	.80
Whole Grain Rye Bread	1 lb. 2 oz.	.70
Whole Wheat Bread	1 lb. 2 oz.	.65
Whole Wheat Frankfurter or Hamburger Buns	each	.12

Deer Valley Farm

Bread Mixes

Vermont General Store and Grist Mill's whole grain flours are stoneground for their own mixes much as the first New England settlers ground flour for their breads and hotcakes. Stonegrinding takes longer and goes slower, but all the grain (the ''whole grain'') stays in the flour, including that supernutritious germ.

Country Graham Quick Bread Mix—stoneground, rich, moist, almost tangy. This bread is delicious toasted for breakfast with coffee. Makes an excellent tea bread. You don't need butter or any other spread to enjoy it. 24-oz. pkg. $1.49

Honey Oatmeal Bread Mix—stoneground whole grain. This is a special favorite. Has the fine flavor of whole grain oats combined with real honey to give it a unique taste. 24-oz. pkg. $1.49

Vermont General Store

Breakfast Cereals

Apple-Cinnamon Granola—made in Penns Creek in small, fresh batches from the following Walnut Acres ingredients: oat flakes, honey, raisins, date sugar, wheat germ, sunflower seeds, peanut oil, dried apples, vanilla, cinnamon, touch of salt. Tasty—not deadly sweet. 1 lb. $.97, 3 lb. $2.79, 5 lb. $4.50

Granny's Granola—made in Walnut Acres from flaked oats, Stern's cane syrup, alfalfa honey, raisins, wheat germ, sesame seeds, chopped apricots, pecan pieces, peanut oil, vanilla, and salt. Baked to perfection. 1 lb. $1.10, 3 lb. $3.09, 5 lb. $5.15

Maple-Almond Granola—another super granola. Made of maple syrup, flaked oats, rye flakes, oat flour, peanut oil, apple juice, raisins, almonds, vanilla extract, cinnamon, and salt.
1 lb. $.96, 3 lb. $2.76, 5 lb. $4.45.

Granola Paks—all granolas above are now packed in individual serving packets. State choice. 2½ oz. $.27 Puffed Millet—ready to eat. 5½-oz. pack. $.78

Walnut Acres

Cooked Breakfast Cereals

Harvest Health offers a variety of stoneground cereals, using the old-fashioned method that consists of two slow-turning stones to grind the grains to desired consistency. Nothing is added, nothing is removed. They believe you will find new pleasure in breakfast when you taste the rich, nutlike flavor of their cereals. Keep them in a cool place for storage and refrigerate during hot, humid weather.

Cream of Rye	22 oz.	$ .89
Dr. Jackson Meal	28 oz.	1.18
Roman Meal (regular)	28 oz.	1.18
Scotch-Style Oatmeal	2 lb.	1.25
Steelcut Oatmeal	2 lb.	1.25

Harvest Health

Whole Grain Cakes

Whole Wheat Angel Cake (no baking powder) sizes vary $1.60 per lb.
Whole Wheat Carob Cake approx. 1½ lb. $1.65 per lb.
Whole Wheat Molasses Cup Cake $1.45 per doz.
Whole Wheat Pound Cake (made with butter), approx. 14 oz. $1.65 per lb.

Deer Valley Farm

Country Fair Candy

This natural organic, carob-covered fruit and nut assortment contains vegetable oil, raw sugar, fruit and nuts, sunflower seeds, blackstrap molasses, cottonseed flour, buttermilk powder, coconut, maple syrup, lecithin, and natural vanilla. No cocoa, chocolate, or cocoa butter is used.

5 oz. sample box $1.50
1-lb. box $3.25

Deer Valley Farm

Coconut

Unlike the highly refined commercial coconut, this does not have the monotonous snow-white color, which is maintained by means of bleaches and chemical acid solutions used before drying. This natural product has flecks of gray and tan throughout, and it has the real coconut taste and odor.

5 lb. $4.50
10 lb. $8.75
25 lb. $21.25

Jaffe Bros.

Cookies and Pastries

All are whole grain and contain no salt.
Butter cookies 1 lb. $1.70
Carob chip cookies 1 doz. $.99
Date-nut bars each $.10, 1 doz. $1.10
Fruit-filled tea ring each $1.25
Oatmeal or sesame cookies 1 doz. $.99

Deer Valley Farm

Dates

These dates are organically grown *and* unfumigated. They are one of the few dates with both these features.
Halawi (semi-moist and flavorful) 5 lb. $3.15, 15 lb. $8.60
Khadrawi (soft) 5 lb. $3.55, 15 lb. $9.60
Zahidi (semi-dry, not too sweet) 5 lb. $2.50, 25 lb. $11.25

Jaffe Bros.

All-Purpose Flour

This is flour made from 100 percent whole, organic winter wheat.

1 lb. $.34
3 lb. $.90
5 lb. $1.35

Walnut Acres

Flaked Grains

Nature Plus is a natural-food supermarket that carries a full spectrum of natural foods including grains, flours, fruit concentrates, nutmeats, oils, soups, syrups, raw sugar, wheat germ, and yeast. They carry the Lima brand in macrobiotic items but suggest that you let them know if they can substitute other brands when Lima is in short supply.

Lima Flaked buckwheat 1 lb. $.99
Lima Flaked millet 1 lb. $.85
Lima Flaked oats 1 lb. $.88
Lima Flaked rice 1 lb. $.89
Lima Flaked rye 1 lb. $.85

Nature Plus

Juices

Biotta juices, imported from Switzerland, are made from organically grown fruits and vegetables only. Choose from tomato juice, beetroot juice, carrot juice, celery juice, orange-banana cocktail, sauerkraut juice, or vegetable cocktail.

17-oz. bottle $1.95 each

Maison Glass

Nut Spreads

Almond Butter—almonds, peanut oil. 8 oz. $2.00

Raw Cashew Butter 3 lb. $6.25; 1 lb. $2.25

Roasted Peanut Butter—made from organically grown federally inspected peanuts. Peanuts are freshly roasted every day—the whole of the peanut—heart, red skin, and all. A little salt is added, but some is made without salt. 1 lb. $1.12; 2 lb. $1.95

Tahini—a sesame seed spread. 1 lb. $1.30

Walnut Acres

Organic Pasta

These items are not made of white flour and contain no bleach, artificial flavoring, colors, or preservatives. Ingredients used are ground vegetable flours, ground soybean flour (40% protein), or whole wheat flours and eggs. They cook up firmly, with old-fashioned homemade goodness. Use at least once or twice a week in taste-tempting casseroles, soups, or salads.

Spinach Egg Noodles 5 oz. $.47
Vegetable Macaroni 11 oz. $.99
Wheat Soy Egg Noodles 5 oz. $.47
Wheat Soy Elbow Macaroni 7 oz.$.46
Wheat Soy Macaroni 7 oz. $.46
Wheat Soy Sea Shells 7 oz. $.46

Harvest Health

Flours and Meals

	3-lb. sack	1-lb. sack
Barley flour (for baking)	$1.80	$.64
Blended bread flour (100% whole wheat from organically raised winter and spring wheat flours)	1.18	.44
Corn meal (100% whole medium)	.93	.35
Muffin meal (100% whole wheat, corn, rye flours only)	.99	.37

Walnut Acres

Natural Oils

These are all Arrowhead Mills brand.

	Quantity	Unit Price	Price
Corn-germ oil	12 pt.	$ .87	$10.44
	12 qt.	1.57	18.84
	1-gal. can		5.10
Olive oil	12 pt.	2.10	25.20
	12 qt.	4.10	49.20
	1-gal. can		14.40
Peanut oil	12 pt.	.96	11.52
	12 qt.	1.80	21.60
Safflower oil	12 pt.	1.10	13.20
	12 qt.	2.10	25.20
	1-gal. can		6.65
Sesame oil	12 pt.	1.25	15.00
	12 qt.	2.35	28.20
	1-gal. can		8.75
Soybean oil	12 pt.	.75	9.00
	12 qt.	1.33	15.00
Sunflower oil	12 pt.	1.02	12.24
	12 qt.	1.87	22.44
Wheat germ oil	12 pt.	2.80	33.60

Erewhon

Pollen

Pollen has from ancient times sustained Olympic athletes, Arab caravans, and the Greeks, Persians, and Chinese. Nutritionally it is a rich source of protein (26%), vitamins, and minerals. Some believe it to be the most nutritious and concentrated food on the planet.

As bees gather pollen from the flower, they form small pellets held together with nectar. Returning to the hive, the bees drop these pellets through a collecting screen. The pollen is then gathered by the beekeeper, to be used as food.

Sprinkle pollen granules on breakfast cereals, sandwiches, ice cream, and other foods. Or blend pollen with honey and water or fruit juice to make a delicious ambrosia.

Bee Pollen from Spain (chamomile and blackberry flowers) 1 lb. $7.00
Bee Pollen from Canada (wilderness flowers) 1 lb. $7.00
Pure Royal Jelly 7000-mg. bottle $7.00

Wonder Natural Foods

Natural Raw Seeds

Millet seed 24 oz. $1.09
Pumpkin seeds (Pepitas) 1 lb. $2.49
Sesame seed 1 lb. $.88
Sunflower seeds 1 lb. $.96

Harvest Health

Dry Soups

Sunshine Valley Vegetable Soup Mix—contains spray-free dried vegetables, almonds, sunflower seeds, sugar, and yeast. With little cooking it makes a satisfying meal—at least 16 meals to a single tin. The contents are "natural," with no water! Try it seasoned with herbs. 8-oz. tin $1.80

Sunshine Valley Garbanzo Soup Mix—similar to the above, but containing garbanzo (chick pea) flour in addition, and with a slightly different flavor. 8-oz. tin $1.80

Walnut Acres

Organic Gift Mailer

This consists of 1 pound of Black Mission figs, 1 pound of Mammoth prunes, 1 pound of Thompson seedless raisins, 12 ounces of unsulphured apricots, and 1 pound of almonds. Everything is organically grown.

1 box $8.95. To Alaska and Hawaii $9.50

Jaffe Bros.

Lacto Brand Yogurt

Fruit flavored 12 oz. $.48. With honey $.50
Plain 12 oz. $.40
Plain 1 qt. $1.18

Deer Valley Farm

Hansen's Acidophilus Culture

This is a ferment made with lactobacillus acidophilus. Although it is thick-textured like yogurt it is called acidophilus milk. It makes an excellent base for salad dressing, or used like sour cream on baked potatoes.

1 culture $2.50

Nichols Garden Nursery

Hansen's Yogurt Culture

This starter makes yogurt that is custardlike in texture with a nutty, mild, almost sweet flavor.

1 starter $2.50

Nichols Garden Nursery

13.

Paté, Caviar, and Truffles

Foie Gras au Naturel

Pure liver from plump overfed Hungarian geese is the only ingredient in this smooth foie gras. Not even a truffle is added to disguise the pure taste. Packed in Strasbourg, the world's paté capital. Just chill and serve.

7-oz. tin $39.95
   3 tins $110.00; 6 tins $200.00

14-oz. tin $69.95
   3 tins $200.00; 6 tins $380.00

21-oz. tin $110.95
   3 tins $300.00; 6 tins $575.00

28-oz. tin $150.00
   3 tins $425.00; 6 tins $800.00

Paprikas Weiss

Bloc de Foie Gras de Canard au Poivre Vert

This foie gras is pure duck liver with green peppercorns. Beautifully gift-boxed.

5-oz. tunnel bloc $15.95
7¼-oz. tunnel bloc $20.95
10¾-oz. tunnel block $30.95

Maison Glass

Parfait Bloc de Foie Gras with Truffles

This is pure French goose liver with truffles in an easy-to-slice tunnel tin. Foie gras de Strasbourg.

The Mail-Order Food Book

15-oz. tin $79.95
3 tins $225.00
Case of 24 tins $1700.00

Paprikas Weiss

French Paté Doré Truffé

This truffled oven-baked paté is a typical French country-style paté brimming with flavor. Foie gras de Strasbourg.

4½-oz. tin $2.50
6 tins $14.00
12 tins $27.00
Case of 50 tins $105.00

Paprikas Weiss

Mousse de Foie Gras Truffée

Light and creamy mousse of goose livers with truffles. Foie gras de Strasbourg.

7-oz. tunnel tin $19.98
   3 tins $58.00
   6 tins $113.00
   Case of 25 tins $437.00
10½-oz. tunnel tin $27.98
   3 tins $82.00
   6 tins $160.00
   Case of 25 tins $625.00

Paprikas Weiss

Roulade de Purée de Foie Dole Truffée

This purée of pure goose-liver paste boasts a center of truffles throughout. Every slice will have truffles in the middle. Foie gras de Strasbourg.

7-oz. tin $14.98, 3 tins $43.00
   6 tins $80.00
   Case of 48 tins $590.00
11-oz. tin $22.98, 3 tins $65.00
   6 tins $127.00
   Case of 30 tins $570.00

Paprikas Weiss

Strasbourg Paté Maison

The original Strasbourg Paté Maison is still carefully prepared to meet all expectations of quality. The finest goose liver is blended with pungent Perigord truffles.

7-oz. tin $5.98
   3 tins $16.00
   Case of 25 tins $112.50
34-oz. tin $19.98
   3 tins $58.00
   Case of 25 tins $405.00

Paprikas Weiss

Térrines de Foie Gras with Truffles

Elegant stone crocks are filled with pure French goose liver with truffles. Foie gras de Strasbourg.

¼-oz. crock $8.98
   3 crocks $25.00
   6 crocks $48.00
4-oz. stone terrine $34.98
   3 terrines $100.00
   6 terrines $190.00
   Case of 24 terrines $705.00

Paprikas Weiss

Five Patés

Here are five different patés you'll be pleased to serve: Cocktail Paté with a subtle flavor, tasty Smoked Turkey Paté, superb Pheasant Supreme, Pate of Smoked Rainbow Trout, and Old-Fashioned Paté of chopped, sautéed chicken livers.

2⅛ oz. $6.75 each

Pepperidge Farm

Fresh Chef-made Paté

	Per lb.
Chicken Liver with Pistachio	$12.00
Duck (smooth and creamy)	10.00
Normande (with Armagnac and apples)	15.00
Provençal (coarse and tangy)	10.00
Supreme (with truffles and pistachios)	12.00
Terrine Canard (with three textures)	15.00
(Minimum shipment 2 lb.)	

Caviarteria

CAVIAR

Beluga Malossol

This is the finest Beluga Malossol caviar—large grain. It is shipped on ice and comes in a jar.

14 oz. $110.00
7 oz. $55.00
3½ oz. $28.00

Maison Glass

Beluga and Sevruga Malossols

Beluga Malossol (Private Stock), large grain:
4-lb. tin per lb. $190.00
14-oz. tin $160.00
7-oz. tin $85.00
8-oz. sealed vacuum jar $95.00
4-oz. sealed vacuum jar $55.00
2-oz. sealed vacuum jar $26.00

Sevruga Malossol (Private Stock), small grain:
4-lb. tin per lb. $125.00
14-oz. tin $115.00
7-oz. tin $60.00
8-oz. sealed vacuum jar $65.00

4-oz. sealed vacuum jar $35.00
2-oz. sealed vacuum jar $19.00

Paprikas Weiss

El Magnifico Assortment

Twelve monthly selections $500.00:
December 14 oz. French Iranian Beluga Malossol caviar
November A 2-lb. side of genuine Scotch smoked salmon on slicing board with knife
October An 11-oz. bloc of Strasbourg foie gras with Perigord truffles
September $25.00 gift certificate for yourself or some lucky associate
August Another $25.00 gift certificate in case you want to defer your choice until later
July & June Three packages each of two fine fish products; a total of six tins of Spanish Filet de Thon and Iceland Baby Brook Trouts
May Three trays of unusual and exquisite party canapes
April A large chunk (about 3 lb.) of smoked sturgeon
March A 3-lb. assortment of exclusive hand-dipped bittersweet chocolates
February Kilo wheel of French Brie cheese, ripe and ready to serve
January A 4-lb. loaf of fresh chef-made duck paté.

Caviarteria

Romanoff

All sturgeon caviar is of Iranian origin.

Iranian and Russian

These caviars are vacuum-packed and keep up to six months.

	1 oz.	2 oz.	4 oz.	8 oz.
Iranian Beluga, giant grain	$4.95	$9.75	$18.95	$37.50
Iranian Sevruga, medium grain	3.95	7.75	15.50	30.00
Russian Kamchatka, broken grain	2.25	4.50	8.95	17.50

Caviarteria

1 oz. Black Seal, large grain $4.50
2 oz. $8.85
1 oz. Blue Seal, pressed $2.85
2 oz. $5.55
1 oz. Green Seal, giant grain $5.00
2 oz. $9.85
1 oz. Red Seal, whole grain $3.80
2 oz. $7.55

Le Jardin du Gourmet

Romanoff Select

Romanoff Select—Black Island Caviar:
24 2-oz. jars (individually boxed) per case $19.98
12 3½-oz. jars (individually boxed) $55.00
12 7-oz. jars $45.00
12 15-oz. jars $69.95

Romanoff Select Red—Iceland Lumpfish Caviar:
12 2-oz jars (individually boxed) per case $19.98
12 3½-oz jars (individually boxed) $29.98
12 7-oz. jars $45.00
12 15-oz. jars $69.95

Paprikas Weiss

Popular Varieties

Beluga Caviar ''Preserved'' (Private Stock) 2-oz. jar $12.95
Caviar (lumpfish) 4-oz. jar $1.95
Cod roe (pressed) 7-oz. tin $1.95
Romanoff Green Seal 2-oz. jar $12.95
Salmon Caviar 4-oz. jar $4.95

Maison Glass

The Mail-Order Food Book

TRUFFLES

White or Black Truffles

Natural Black Truffles ⅞-oz. jar. $8.75
1¾-oz. jar. $19.50
White Truffles ½-oz. jar $7.50
1-oz. jar $15.00

Maison Glass

French Truffles

These are the finest imported from France. Truffles are an aromatic, flavorsome fungus of the tuber family.

⅞-oz. tin $6.10

Le Jardin du Gourmet

14.

Hickory Smoked Chicken

These meaty birds have the same spicy flavor and pink meat as smoked turkey. Smoked the "Ozark way," with real mountain hickory wood, this ready-to-eat delicacy makes a thoughtful gift for the holidays or just to say "thank you" any time of year.

2 chickens per package $8.00
3 chickens per package $11.00
4 chickens per package $14.00
6 chickens per package $19.00
12 chickens per package $35.00
All prices postpaid in continental U.S.

Ozark Mountain Smoke House

The Mail-Order Food Book

More Hickory Smoked Chicken

Tender birds, slowly smoked to retain their natural juices while imparting old-fashioned goodness. More delicate than turkey, they are carefully prepared to bring out their elegant flavor. An ideal leisure-time offering. Shipped October through March.

2 2-lb. chickens $12.95

Omaha Steaks International

Smoked Duck

Pure wood-smoked duck that arrives fully cooked and ready to eat, with slicing and serving suggestions. A brace of two ducks may also be ordered. Available September through April.

2¾ to 3¼ lb.
Single $10.95
Brace $18.95

Figi's

More Smoked Duck

Delicious whole duck that is gently cured and slow smoked for the very finest flavor. Arrives fully cooked. A rare delicacy and delightful gift; a unique taste experience.

3 lb. (minimum) $11.95

The Swiss Colony

B&B Smoked Turkey

Smoked Turkey—a real scene-stealer for your holiday buffet, garden party, or special Sunday dinner. This glistening bronze-toned beauty has the true turkey flavor—but with an extra dimension in taste: it's cured with molasses and spice and smoked with hickory to embellish its distinct turkey identity. It is tender and succulent right down to the makings of flavorful turkey soup. And it arrives fully cooked and ready to serve. Approx. 10 lb. $23.70 to $25.90 depending on delivery area.

Smoked Turkey Breast—like the whole smoked turkey, this breast is cured to perfection with molasses and delicately smoked to enhance the flavor. Here is the succulent white meat of the turkey, fully cooked and so easy to carve! Approx. 5 lb. $19.30 to $20.40 depending on delivery area.

Broadbent B&B Food Products

Grade A Smoked Turkey

These are plump, broad-breasted U.S. Grade A turkeys smoked to a luscious brown for "down on the farm" country flavor and tenderness. Available September through April.

5–6 lb. $14.95
8½–9½ lb. $19.95

Figi's

Harry and David Smoked Turkey

Here's a holiday party all ready to serve and savor hot or cold. Only "sweet" extra-tender birds are selected for this special slow smoking that produces a bird of tantalizing smokiness. Large turkey weighs 9½ to 10½ pounds.

Order Gift No. 382 $26.95 delivered

Harry and David

Hickory Smoked Turkey

Turkey is ready to carve, serve, and enjoy. From the heart of the Arkansas Ozarks, this turkey with its pearly pink meat and incomparable taste has been a favorite of gourmets for years. For formal dinners or the cold-meat platter, this smoked turkey adds flair to your entertaining.

Extra small hen 8½–9½ lb. $19.50
Small hen 9½–10½ lb. $21.50
Medium hen 10½–11½ lb. $23.00
Large hen 11½–12½ lb. $25.00
Extra large hen 12½–13½ lb. $27.00

Ozark Mountain Smoke House

Smoked Boneless Turkey Breast

A turkey breast that is boned, cured, smoked, and fully cooked—just slice and serve. Paper-thin slices are great for sandwiches or canapés; thicker slices for a main course. Either way there is no waste to this all-white-meat breast.

3½–4½ lb. $19.00

Ozark Mountain Smoke House

Omaha Smoked Turkey

These are completely cooked, unusually tender birds delicately prepared to bring out their elegant flavor. They are slowly smoked to retain their natural juices while imparting an old-fashioned goodness. Shipped October through March.

9–10 lb. $22.50

Omaha Steaks International

Smokehouse Turkey

This ready-to-serve whole smoked turkey is plump and broad-breasted. Each turkey is carefully selected and processed according to Braunfels' time-proved recipe—hand rubbed, slowly bin cured, and smoked. Each turkey is outstanding for its tender, moist, smoky goodness. Ready to carve, serve, and enjoy.

10–20 lb. $2.35 per lb.

The New Braunfels Smokehouse

Turkey Breast or Whole Smoked Turkey

Choose either the turkey breast or a whole bird; both are moist and tasty. Comes already smoked, ready to eat, easy to slice.

4½-lb. breast $19.95
10-lb. turkey $28.95

Pepperidge Farm

The Mail-Order Food Book

Game Birds

Mallard Ducks or Pheasants

These excellent birds are game-farm raised and NPIP tested and certified. Each bird weighs between 2 and 2½ pounds. When served with wild rice, each provides a truly succulent meal. Either ''brace of birds'' is packaged in dry ice and shipped via United Parcel Service to Minnesota and bordering states and by airmail to all others.

Mallard brace $32.50
Pheasant brace $32.50
Airmail: add $4.00 for the first brace and $2.00 for each additional brace

Gokeys

Partridge

A whole partridge from Scotland.

15½-oz. tin $9.00

Maison Glass

Pheasants

These are plump, meaty birds that have been raised on a diet chock full of grain, which imparts a delicate flavor reminiscent of wild pheasants but without the gaminess. Young and full-breasted birds, meticulously cleaned. Available October 1 through January 1 if supply lasts.

4 pheasants, each 23–27 oz. $38.00

Omaha Steaks International

Hickory-smoked Pheasant

Harry and David's famous hickory-smoking method makes this gourmet bird's white meat taste as subtle as a delicate wine—and the dark meat taste like ham cured real southern style. Each 2- to 2½-pound pheasant is delightful as a main course, with stealings left over. An

elegant gift for the most special friends on your list.

Order Gift No. 383 $15.95 delivered

Harry and David

Maison Glass Pheasant

Whole Smoked Ringneck Pheasant 3-lb. tin $12.95
Whole Pheasant in Wine Sauce (Scotland) 3-lb. tin $14.95

Maison Glass

Smoked Pheasant

This whole smoked bird is a gourmet's delight.

2½ lb. $17.95

Pepperidge Farm

Smoked Ringneck Pheasant

Only plump, juicy pheasants, cured and smoked to lend a most unusual delicate flavor, are shipped. They make a royal delicacy, perfect for the holidays.

Net wt. 2⅛ lb. $11.95

The Swiss Colony

Quail

Originally Asian game birds, these plump, white-skinned quail are raised on domestic prairie lands. Their flavor is rich and savory without being gamey. Omaha recommends a brace of quail per serving. Easy cooking and serving instructions are enclosed with order.

8 4- to 6-oz. quail $33.50
12 4- to 6-oz. quail $43.50

Omaha Steaks International

Wild Birds

Chukar Partridge average 16 oz. each $8.50

Mallard Ducks average 2 lb. per lb. $4.40

Pheasants average 3 lb. per lb. $4.50

Quail (Bob White) average 6 oz. each $3.95

Wild Turkeys average 10–12 lb. per lb. $4.75

Maison Glass

The Mail-Order Food Book

15.

PUDDINGS

Addison's Christmas Puddings

Addison's famous old-fashioned Christmas Puddings are made with Barley Wine and Rum and supplied in plastic basins.

3 14-oz. puddings $11.90
2 1 lb. 7 oz. puddings $11.76
2 1 lb. 12 oz. puddings $13.30

Egertons

F & M Christmas Pudding

F & M Christmas Pudding is made to their own recipe. Each pudding is packed in a specially designed container for safe delivery. They come in several sizes; prices are approximate.

2 lb. $7.00. Post and packing $2.50
3 lb. $10.00. Post and packing $3.00
4 lb. $12.00. Post and packing $3.00

6 lb. $17.00. Post and packing $4.00
8 lb. $25.00. Post and packing $6.00

Fortnum & Mason

Harry & David's Christmas Pudding

Here's a traditionally dark, dark pudding to be served steaming and fragrant. It is rich with plump currants, raisins, English walnuts, fresh creamery butter, and tantalizing spices. Included are easy instructions for heating and serving, plus the recipe for Harry's Tried 'n True Hard Sauce. Cellophane wrapped in cheery red-and-white gingham and tied with a pretty bow, it'll be a merry addition to the Christmas table.

Order Gift No. 339 $8.95 delivered

Harry and David

Holiday Pudding

Moist and fluffy cake, resplendent with fruits and nuts, comes gift wrapped with its shiny reusable mold. Included is 8 ounces of Special Brandy Butter Cream, enough to cover every individual slice

generously. Comes with easy instructions to serve hot or cold.

Net wt. 18 oz. $7.25

The Swiss Colony

Indian Pudding

This old New England favorite comes tinned and ready to serve either hot or cold.

15-oz. can $1.00

Especially Maine

Plum Pudding

From Fortnum & Mason comes Export Box ''A.'' Included with the Christmas Plum Pudding is a tin of Old English Fruit Cake, Royal Blend Tea, Crystallised Ginger, English Breakfast Marmalade, Old English Mincemeat, and other goodies.

Assortment above $32.33 U.S.
$32.00 Canada

Fortnum & Mason

Lemon Hart Plum Pudding

Made with the best of all the traditional ingredients with the addition of Lemon Hart Rum from Jamaica, this is a plum pudding with a luscious flavor.

Net wt. 2 lb.

Egertons

Prices
obtainable on
request from
supplier.

16.

SOUPS

Bouillabaisse

This soup has an Hungarian accent! An authentic fish soup in a cube livened with Hungarian paprika. Just add water, then add your favorite fish or seafood, and *voila!* The extra "kick" is the paprika, the genuine Hungarian flavoring that adds spicy tang and rich color to all cooking.

2 cubes $1.50
Box of 20 cubes $13.00

Paprikas Weiss

Clam Chowder

This is the traditional Cape Ann delicacy made from an authentic "seafaring forefathers" recipe used in fishing-boat galleys. Each can of condensed clam chowder should be mixed with an equal portion of milk. Serve steaming hot!

3 15-oz. cans $2.95
6 15-oz. cans $5.95

Embassy Seafoods

Fish Chowder

Fresher-than-fresh fish from the Gulf of Maine, cooked to perfection with potatoes, onions, and sprightly seasoning, go into this chowder. Just add milk and serve. Makes about a quart per tin.

6 15-oz. tins $7.40

Saltwater Farm

Haddock Chowder

Fresh chunks of selected haddock, potatoes, onions, milk, flour, and spices are combined in Embassy's condensed Haddock Chowder. Add an equal portion of milk, heat and serve.

3 15-oz. cans $3.05
6 15-oz. cans $6.00

Embassy Seafoods

Fruit Soups

Here's a Scandinavian surprise so versatile that you can serve it as a meal starter or crown your dinner with Fruit Soup for dessert. Full-color 28-page booklet of recipes is included. Includes two cans each of bing cherry with Burgundy, peach-apple, and orange with apricot, one can each of strawberry with Sauterne and prune with orange.

8 11-oz. cans $8.95

Pepperidge Farm

New Orleans Soups

Gumbo, crayfish bisque, and turtle soup are packed in a gift box. Two of each flavor come in a box. These are soups for the gourmet.

6 10-oz. cans $9.95

Kate Latter's

Onion Soup Gourmet

Semi-condensed French onion soup is combined with traditional onion-soup bowls. *Très bien!* Handcrafted bowls are of natural, stoneware pottery hand-dipped in glaze the old-fashioned way. Bowls are ovenproof and complete with covers.

2 soups, 2 bowls $8.95
4 soups, 4 bowls $15.95

Pepperidge Farm

Seafood Soups

Package contains two cans each of

New England clam chowder and Maryland crab soup; one can each of lobster bisque and oyster stew. Semi-condensed.

6 cans $8.95

Pepperidge Farm

Variety Soups

Black Bean with Sherry Wine	13-oz. tin	$ .75
Clater Consomme	13-oz. tin	.75
Cream of Onion Soup (Soubise)	13-oz. tin	.75
Cream of Senegalese	13-oz. tin	.75
Cream of Vichyssoise	13-oz. tin	.75
Gazpacho	13-oz. tin	.75
Green Turtle Consomme with Sherry Wine	13-oz. tin	.85
She-Crab (condensed)	11½-oz. tin	1.25
Turtle & Pea (Boula)	13-oz. tin	.85
Shark's Fin Soup	15 oz. tin	2.75
Bird's Nest Soup	15 oz. tin	3.50

Maison Glass

The Mail-Order Food Book

17.

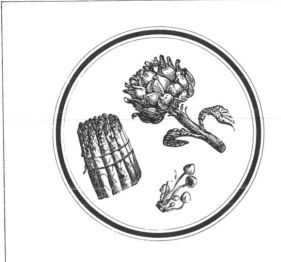

VEGETABLES

artichokes

large size

California Artichokes

From the fertile coastal fields of California, near Monterey Bay, come luscious, exotic artichokes. Whether large or small, they have the same mouth-watering goodness when they are boiled and eaten as finger foods. Small artichokes are better for pickling, or for salads and casseroles; large ones are great for stuffing and as the main course of a meal. Although picked and packed fresh from the field all year long, prices vary by season.

24 small artichokes, each 2½″ in diameter $9.00 west of Mississippi $12.50 east of Mississippi

12 large artichokes, each 4″ diameter $9.00 west of Mississippi $12.50 east of Mississippi

Boggiato Packing

Imported Artichokes

Import from France: 14¾-oz. tin (6–8 count) $1.90
12-oz. tin (10–12 count) $1.95

Import from Spain (artichoke hearts in brine):
7-oz. tin (6–8 count) $.55
14-oz. tin (8–10 count) $.95

Le Jardin du Gourmet

State o' Maine Baking Beans

Yellow Eye, Soldier, or Jacob's Cattle, whatever your favorite combination of pork, mustard, and molasses, quality beans still are important. These are superb for the traditional Maine Saturday night fare.

2 lb. $2.00

Especially Maine

Dandelion Greens

These are historically Maine's first vegetable crop (along with fiddleheads) each spring. These succulent and tender greens can now be enjoyed year-round.

15-oz. can $1.25

Especially Maine

Fiddlehead Greens

These are historically Maine's first vegetable crop (along with dandelions) each spring. These succulent and tender greens can now be enjoyed year-round.

15-oz. can $1.25

Especially Maine

Flageolets

These are dry green beans, the traditional partner of roast leg of lamb.

17-oz. box $1.65

Le Jardin du Gourmet

Arrowhead Beans

	Quantity & Size		Price
Alfalfa Seeds	12	1-lb.	$20.20
Black-Eyed Peas	12	24-oz.	9.00
Chickpeas	12	1-lb.	8.80
Lentils	12	1-lb.	6.30
Lima	12	24-oz.	8.60
Mung Beans	12	1-lb.	7.70
Pinto Beans	12	1-lb.	5.90
Sesame Seeds	12	12-oz.	9.50
Shelled Raw Peanuts	18	1-lb.	15.10
Soybeans	12	1-lb.	3.50
Split Peas	12	1-lb.	4.40
Sunflower Seeds	12	12-oz.	9.70

Arrowhead Mills

Beans and Chilis

Casa Moneo, because of its Spanish-derivative orientation, carries a wide variety of beans and chilis.

Item	Brand	Size	Price
Chili or Beans	Austex	15½ oz.	$ .33
Chili Con Carne	Old El Paso	15 oz.	.97
Dried Chiles	La Victoria	1 lb.	1.80
Dried Pasilla Chiles	La Victoria	1 lb.	3.00
Green Chili	Gebhardts	4 oz.	.35
Mexe Beans	Old El Paso	15 oz.	.27
Refried Beans	La Victoria	20 oz.	.45

Casa Moneo

Erewhon Beans

Azuki Beans	25 lb.	$10.00
Chickpeas (Garbanzos)	25 lb.	11.00
Green Lentils	25 lb.	7.50
	100 lb.	27.00
Green Split Peas	25 lb.	5.00
Organic Mung Beans	25 lb.	11.00
Organic Pinto Beans	25 lb.	10.00
Organic Soybean Flakes	25 lb.	6.50

Erewhon

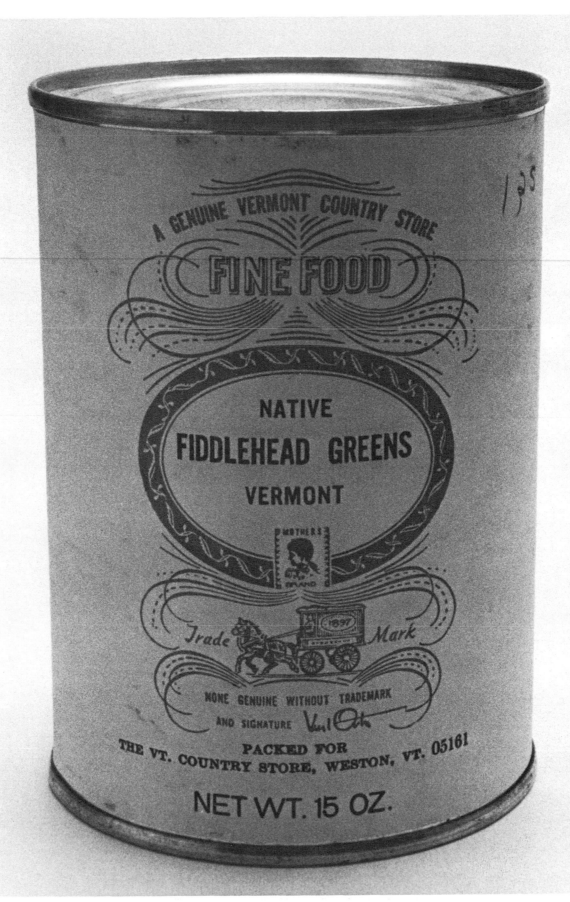

A GENUINE VERMONT COUNTRY STORE

FINE FOOD

NATIVE
FIDDLEHEAD GREENS
VERMONT

Trade   Mark

NONE GENUINE WITHOUT TRADEMARK
AND SIGNATURE

PACKED FOR
THE VT. COUNTRY STORE, WESTON, VT. 05161

NET WT. 15 OZ.

Le Jardin du Gourmet Mushrooms

Drained wt. 8 oz. Ship weight 16 oz.
$3.45

Le Jardin du Gourmet

Maison Glass Mushrooms

Button Mushrooms 4-oz. tin $1.00
Button Mushrooms 8-oz. tin $1.95
Cepes 10-oz. tin $5.95
Chanterelles 8-oz. tin $5.95
Freeze Dried, whole (France)
7/10-oz. tin $2.50
Freeze Dried, sliced (France) ½-oz.
tin $2.50
Morels, dried (Switzerland) 1-oz.
box $4.50

Maison Glass

Hickin's Shallots

Large size: 5 oz. $1.19; 1 lb. $3.25

Hickin's

Shallots

Ship ¾ pound anywhere in the
United States for only $2.00
postpaid. Receive them monthly (for
one year) for $20.00; or bimonthly
for $10.00. By the pound, when part
of a food order, $1.75 plus postage.

Le Jardin du Gourmet

Assorted Sea Vegetables

Agar agar—a sea gelatin that can be
used to make desserts or salad molds,
or in dishes where a thickener is
desired. 20 1-oz. $16.00

Dulse—delicate, tangy flavor unlike
any other sea or land vegetable. Rich
in minerals, it can be served raw in
salads or cooked in soups. 24 2-oz.
$14.00

Kiziki—harvested in the Sea of
Japan, selected and dried by hand;
high in minerals, particularly iodine
and iron. 10 2¾-oz. $8.50

Kombu—sweet and delicate in taste.
Kombu is often used as a base for
soups. Grown off the northern tip of
Japan, it is known to be nutritionally
one of the richest seaweeds. 10
2¾-oz. $8.20

Nori—a thin sheet of sun-dried kelp
that is great for making rice balls and
sushi. Roast as a garnish for a real
treat. 10 2¾-oz. $8.50

Wakame—deep green in color.
Wakame grows in late winter and
early spring as the sea begins to
warm. Delicious in soups or cooked
with other vegetables. 10 2¾-oz.
$8.00

Erewhon

Hijiki, Kombu, Wakame Sea Vegetables

These plants are not to be confused
with the common sea kelp found in
shallow and more southerly waters.
They are generally used in soups, but
also lend their unique flavors easily
to sautéed, steamed, or
pressure-cooked vegetables. Write to
supplier for current prices.

Chico-San

East Wind Chinese Specialties

East Wind specializes in items from
China and sells food and spices, bean
cake, noodles, canned and preserved
fruit, tea, and candy.

Bamboo Shoots 6-oz. can $.65
Fried Fish Paste 8-oz. can $1.30
Kumquat 11-oz. can $.85
Lychee (in syrup) 20-oz. can $1.50
Mushrooms 8-oz. can $1.25
Rice Cakes 21-oz. bag $1.25
Spiced Vegetables 10½-oz. jar $.95

East Wind

Maison Glass Chinese Specialties

Bamboo Shoots 20-oz. tin $1.50
Ginger in Syrup 9½-oz. jar $1.95
Green Ginger (sliced) 4½-oz. tin
$1.50
Lychee Nuts in Syrup 11-oz. tin
$1.25
Soy Sauce 10-oz. btl. $1.10
Water Chestnuts 12-oz. tin $1.50
(Pickled) Water Chestnuts 9½-oz. jar
$1.50

Maison Glass

18.

MIXED BAG

Couscous

Made of durum wheat, this North African specialty arrives precooked.

17-oz. $1.15

Le Jardin du Gourmet

Egg White Powder

Nothing is used but egg whites powdered for convenience and economy. Simply dissolve powdered pure egg albumen in water and whip up as you would fresh egg whites.

½ lb. $2.35

Maid of Scandinavia

Indonesian Foods

Bumbu—a powdered spice mixture for special dishes: Bali, Bebotok, Godok, Opor, Rudjak 1 jar $.65
Djambu Kelutuk—pitted guava halves 30-oz. tin $1.15
Emping Melindjo—vegetable wafers, to deep-fry 7 oz. $2.20
Ketimoen—cucumber relish 12 oz. $1.50
Ketjap Benteng—Java soy sauce 1 pt. $2.40. 1 qt. $4.80
Krup Udang—shrimp-tapioca wafers, to deep-fry. A ''must'' with rice. 4 oz. $1.00. 1 lb. $3.60
Sambal—hot chili pepper paste:
  Sambal Ulek (red, not fried) small $.70. 7-oz. $2.00
  Sambal Asem (fried incl. tamarind) small $.70

Mrs. De Wildt

Vanilla

''Hand-made'' vanilla flavoring from the Dolan Company is made in the same oaken vats and bottled with the same labels as when the company was founded at the turn of the century. Contains only 3 percent alcohol. The flavor will not cook out.

4 oz. $.75
16 oz. $.25 per oz.

Especially Maine

Vine Leaves

These are imported vine leaves packed in brine, for stuffing.

16-oz. bottle $1.65

Lekvar By The Barrel

Mulled Wine Spices

''Gluhfix'' is a wonderfully tasting drink from Dusseldorf that dates from earliest times. Add it to red wine, then heat and taste history. Fifteen individual envelopes of spice assure a perfect Gluhfix every time.

1 pkg. $1.60

Calico Kitchen

Red Star Baker's Yeast

This fresh dried yeast has been bulk packed for economy. It has tremendous leavening power. Comes in a reusable plastic jar for easy refrigeration.

1 lb. $2.25

Nichols Garden Nursery

Seeds: Sprouting Kits

Take your choice—one, two, or all. These magic sprouting kits are the result of many months of testing and experimenting. Each 5½″ x 8″ terrarium sprouting kit contains seed, seed bed, sprouting chart, serving suggestions, and recipes. All you do is add water to seed bed, sprinkle on seeds, replace cover, and watch them grow. In as little as 22 hours, depending on the seed variety, your sprouts will be ready to harvest and eat.

Sprouting Kits	Each	Cost for 2	Cost for 2 Extra Seeds
Alfalfa	$2.50	$4.00	$2.50
Fenugreek	2.50	4.00	2.50
Lentils	2.50	4.00	2.50
Mung Beans	2.50	4.00	2.50
Peas	2.50	4.00	2.50
Wheat	2.50	4.00	2.50

Sourdough Jack's

The Mail-Order Food Book

Food Catalogue Directory

Amana Society
Meat Dept.
Amana, Iowa 52203
Meat variety packages, smoked ham, bacon and sausage

Aphrodisia
28 Carmine Street
New York, New York 10014
Herbs, spices, seasonings and flavorings

The Appleyard Corporation
Maple Corner
Calais, Vermont 05648
Cheese, cereals, condiments, maple syrup, mixes

Arrowhead Mills
Box 866
Hereford, Texas 79045
Flours, vegetables, beans, whole grains

Ault Bee Farm
Box 23
Route 3, Weslaco, Texas 78596
Honey, preserves

Bailey's of Boston
26 Temple Place
Boston, Massachusetts 02111
Candies

Birkett Mills
P.O. Box 440
Penn Yan, New York 14527
Flour, grains

Bissinger's
205 West Fourth Street
Cincinnati, Ohio 45202
Candies, cookies

Boggiato Packing Co.
"Mr. Artichoke"
11000 Blackie Road
Castroville, California 95012
Artichokes

Briggsway Co.
Ugashik, Alaska 99683
Salmon: canned in glass, smoked, spread

Broadbent B&B Food Products
Route 1
Cadiz, Kentucky 42211
Fruitcake, smoked bacon, ham, sausage, turkey

Brookside Farm
Turnbridge, Vermont 05077
Maple syrup

Butterfield Farms, Inc.
8500 Wilshire Boulevard
Suite 1005
Beverly Hills, California 90211
Fruitcake

Byrd Cookie Co.
P.O. Box 13086
Savannah, Georgia 31406
Candies, cookies

Byrd Mills Co.
P.O. Box 5167
Richmond, Virginia 23220
Cookies, flours, whole grains

Calico Kitchens
P.O. Box 2452
San Francisco, California 94126
Fruit and nut butters, candies, condiments, honey, nuts, sourdough bread

Caravel Coffee Co.
P.O. Box 554
Jackson Heights, New York 11372
Coffee, tea

Casa Moneo
210 West 14th Street
New York, New York 10011
Herbs, spices, vegetables, Mexican and Spanish foods

Caviarteria
870 Madison Avenue
New York 10021
Caviar, cheese, paté

Celestial Seasonings
P.O. Box 1405
Boulder, Colorado 80302
Herbal teas

Happy Gifts of Food from Old New Orleans...

PACKED WITH LOVING CARE BY
CREOLE DELICACIES CO., INC.

chico-san inc. products

A CATALOGUE OF UNIQUE FOODS

Diamond Goat Farm

presents

• NATURAL
• DELICIOUS
• NUTRITIOUS

MILK

healthful
GOAT MILK
and
GOAT CHEESE

CONTACT YOUR LOCAL HEALTH FOOD SUPPLIER

R. H. Chamberlin
Box 87
Sharpes, Florida 32959
Fresh fruits, fish, shellfish

Chico-San, Inc.
P.O. Box 1004
Chico, California 95926
Nut and fruit butters, cookies, biscuits, rice, syrup, organic and natural foods, herbal teas

O. H. Clapp & Co.
47 Riverside Avenue
Westport, Connecticut 06880
Tea

Collin Street Bakery
Box 79
Corsicana, Texas 75110
Fruitcake

Crawford Lobster Co.
Badgers Island
Kittery, Maine 03904
Fillets of cod and mackerel, live lobster

Creole Delicacies Co.
533 St. Ann Street
New Orleans, Louisiana 70116
Condiments

Dakin Farm
Route 7
Ferrisburg, Vermont 05456
Cheese, maple syrup

Deer Valley Farm
R.D. 1
Guilford, New York 13780
Organic foods, yogurt

Mrs. De Wildt
RFD 3
Bangor, Pennsylvania 18013
Indonesian foods

Food Catalogue Directory

Shopping in Britain by mail

Egertons Postal Gift & Shopping Service 1976-77

Unsurpassed Cup Quality

Grace Rare Tea

EDEN FOODS

SPRING CATALOG 1976

Diamond Dairy Goat Farm
Route 2
Portage, Wisconsin 53901
Cheese

East Wind
2801 Broadway
New York, New York 10025
Chinese foods

Eden Foods
Box 100
Ann Arbor, Michigan 48107
Natural and organic foods

Egerton's
5 Fore Street
Seaton
Devon EX122LB, England
Cakes, candies, cookies, biscuits, tea cakes, honey, preserves, puddings

Embassy Foods
P.O. Box 165
Gloucester, Massachusetts 01930
Cheese, maple syrup, smoked salmon, cod and mackerel fillets, canned shad roe, shellfish, soups

Empire Coffee & Tea Co.
486 Ninth Avenue
New York, New York 10018
Coffee, tea

Erewhon Trading Co.
8454 Steller Drive
Culver City, California 90230
Nut and fruit butters, flours, dried fruits, herbs, spices, seasonings, flavorings, herbal teas, vegetables, sea vegetables, whole grains

Especially Maine
Vinegar Hill Road
Arundel, Maine 04046
Blueberries, maple syrup, puddings, vegetables, beans, dandelion greens, fiddleheads

Fauchon's
24 Place de la Madeleine
Paris-75008, France
Candies, paté, preserved fruits in cordials

Figi's
Marshfield, Wisconsin 54449
Cakes, cheese, smoked duck, dried fruits, fresh fruits, honey, ham, sausage, nuts, pastries, preserves, smoked turkey

The Fmali Co.
P.O. Box 1072
Santa Cruz, California 95061
Herbs, spices, herbal teas

Fortnum & Mason
Picadilly
London W1A1ER, England
Cakes, candies, honey, puddings, mincemeat

Gokey's
21 West Fifth Street
St. Paul, Minnesota 55102
Smoked pheasant, wild rice

Golden Acres Orchard
Box 70
Front Royal, Virginia 22630
Fresh apples

Graber Olive House
Box 511
Ontario, California 91761
Dried fruits, dates, nuts, olives

Grace Tea Co.
799 Broadway
New York, New York 10003
Tea

Great Valley Mills
101 South West End Boulevard
Quakertown, Pennsylvania 18951
Cakes, cookies, fruitcake, smoked ham, bacon, sausage, bologna, scrapple

Green Mountain Sugar House
RFD 1
Ludlow, Vermont 05149
Cheese, honey, maple syrup, maple sugar, pancake mix

John Harman's Store
Sugar Hill, New Hampshire 03585
Cheddar cheese

Harry and David
Bear Creek Orchards
Medford, Oregon 97501
Cakes, candies, cheese, fruitcake, dried fruits, fresh fruits, smoked pheasant, smoked turkey, nuts, pastries, preserves, puddings

Harvest Health, Inc.
1944 Eastern Avenue S.E.
Grand Rapids, Michigan 49507
Herbs, spices, natural and organic foods

Harvey's Groves
Box 430
Cocoa, Florida 32922
Fresh fruits

Harwood Hill Orchard
Route 7 North
Bennington, Vermont 05201
Cheese, condiments, apples, honey, maple syrup, apple syrup

Hegg & Hegg
801 Marine Drive
Port Angeles, Washington 98362
Smoked salmon, seafood

The Herb Lady
P.O. Box 26515
Los Angeles, California 90026
Herbs, spices

Herb Product Co.
11012 Magnolia Boulevard.
North Hollywood, California 91601
Herbs

Mrs. Herbst Pastry & Strudel, Inc.
1437 Third Avenue
New York, New York 10028
Strudels, tortes

Hickin's
Black Mountain Road
Brattleboro, Vermont 05301
Fruitcake, honey, maple syrup, fruit syrups, preserves, shallots

Icemart
Keflavik International Airport
Iceland
Seafood

Indiana Botanic Gardens
P.O. Box 5
Hammond, Indiana 46325
Herbs, spices

Infinity Co.
173 Duane Avenue
New York, New York 10005
Flours, herbs, spices, pasta, whole grains

Jaffe Bros.
P.O. Box 636
Valley Center, California 92082
Natural and organic foods

Iceland's finest Products at

ICEMART

MAIL ORDER AND SHOPPING GUIDE 1975-76

V. W. Joyner & Co.
315 Main Street
Smithfield, Virginia 23430
Smoked bacon, ham

Kakawateez, Ltd.
130 Olive Street
Findlay, Ohio 45840
Nuts

Kate Latter's
300 Royal Street
New Orleans, Louisiana 70130
Candies, cakes, coffee, condiments,
fruitcake, preserves, soups

Kemoo Farm Foods
P.O. Box 236
Lodi, California 95240
Cakes, candies, fruitcake, preserves

Koinonia Products
Route 2
Americus, Georgia 31709
Candies, cereals, fruitcake, nuts

Lang Apiaries
Gasport, New York 14067
Honey

Lawrence Smoke House
Route 30
Newfane, Vermont 05348
Smoked bacon, ham, honey, cheese,
maple syrup

Le Jardin du Gourmet
Les Echalottes
West Danville, Vermont 05873
Candies, caviar, condiments, herbs,
spices, mushrooms, polenta, snails,
truffles, shallots

Lekvar By The Barrel
H. Roth & Son
1577 First Avenue
New York, New York 10028
Nut and fruit butters, condiments, herbs,
spices, snails

Magic Herb Garden
P.O. Box 332
Fairfax, California 94930
Herbs, spices

Maid of Scandinavia
3244 Raleigh Avenue
Minneapolis, Minnesota 55416
Candies, mixes

Maison Glass
52 East 58th Street
New York, New York 10022
Caviar, cheese, condiments, cookies,
biscuits, herbs, spices, mushrooms,
smoked partridge, tinned paté, snails,
truffles, tea

Manganaro Foods
488 Ninth Avenue
New York, New York 10028
Cakes, candies, cheese, herbs, spices,
honey, pasta, preserves

McArthur's Smokehouse, Inc.
Millerton, New York 12546
Smoked ham

McNulty's Tea and Coffee Co.
109 Christopher Street
New York, New York 10014
Coffee, regular tea, herbal teas

Minnehaha Wild Rice Co.
420 WCCO Radio Building
Minneapolis, Minnesota 55402
Wild rice

Nature Plus
125 First Avenue
New York, New York 10003
Flours, organic and natural foods, whole
grains

Nature's Herb Co.
281 Ellis Street
San Francisco, California 94102
Herbs, spices

The New Braunfels Smokehouse
P.O. Box 1159
New Braunfels, Texas 78130
Smoked meats, smoked turkey

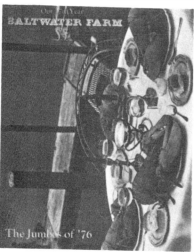

Nichols Garden Nursery
1190 North Pacific Highway
Albany, Oregon 97321
Cheese, condiments, herbs, spices, sourdough starter, herbal teas

Northern Health Foods
P.O. Box 66
Moorehead, Minnesota 56560
Flours, nuts, natural and organic foods, whole grains

Northwestern Coffee Mills
217 North Broadway
Milwaukee, Wisconsin 53202
Coffee, tea, herbs, spices, wild rice

Omaha Steaks, International
4400 South 96th Street
Omaha, Nebraska 68127
Beef, ham steaks, lamb, pork sausage, veal, smoked chicken, pheasant, quail, smoked salmon, shellfish, St. Peter's fish

Ozark Mountain Smoke House Inc.
P.O. Box 37
Farmington, Arkansas 72730
Smoked bacon, pork loin, ham, sausage, turkey

The Packing Shed
P.O. Box 11
Weyers Cave, Virginia 24486
Hams, nuts

Paprikas Weiss
1546 Second Avenue
New York, New York 10028
Candies, caviar, dried fruits, herbs, spices, honey, coffee, tea, tinned meats, pasta, mixes

Pepperidge Farm Mail Order Co.
P.O. Box 119
Clinton, Connecticut 06413
Nut and fruit butters, cakes, candies, cookies, fruitcake, dried fruits, maple syrup, smoked pheasant, ham, bacon, pastries

Pete's Dates
P.O. Box 863
Camarillo, California 93010
Dried and stuffed dates, nuts

Plumbridge
33 East 61st Street
New York, New York 10021
Candies, nuts

Priester's Pecans
227 Old Fort Drive
Fort Deposit, Alabama 36032
Candies, fruitcake, nuts

Rancher Waltenspiel
4791 Dry Creek Road
Healdsburg, California 95448
Dried fruits

Rebecca-Ruth Candy
112 East Second Street
Frankfort, Kentucky 40601
Candies

Ritchie Bros
37 Watergate
Rothesay
Isle of Bute, Scotland
Smoked salmon

Rocky Hollow Herb Farm
R.D. 2, Box 215
Lake Wallkill Road
Sussex, New Jersey 07461
Herbs, spices, tea

Saltwater Farm
Varrell Lane
York Harbor, Maine 03911
Live lobster, smoked salmon, soups, shellfish

Schaller & Weber Inc.
22-25 46th Street
Long Island City, New York 11105
Smoked sausages, hams, meats

Schapira Coffee Co.
117 West Tenth Street
New York, New York 10011
Coffee, tea

Now you are invited to enjoy
A Natural Old-Fashioned
VERMONT
COUNTRY
BREAKFAST

Vermont general store & grist mill

A unique selection of easy to prepare
Wholegrain Pancake & Muffin Mixes
&
Pure Vermont Maple Syrup.

Delicious Delectable
OREGON
PRUNES
with that DELIGHTFUL TASTE difference!

Ready to Eat

FAMOUS
for
FLAVOR

47 Years

GROWN, TENDERIZED, AND PACKED BY
SUNRAY ORCHARDS
OF MYRTLE CREEK, OREGON 97457
Rt. 1 Box No. 299   Phone: 839-4116

Shiloh Farms
Box 97
Sulphur Springs, Arizona 72768
Natural and organic foods

Simpson & Vail
53 Park Place
New York, New York 10007
Coffee, tea

Smithfield Ham Products Co.
P.O. Box 487
Smithfield, Virginia 23430
Bacon, ham

Sourdough Jack's
P.O. Box 40218
San Francisco, California 94140
Sourdough starter, beef jerky

Sternberg Pecan Co.
P.O. Box 193
Jackson, Mississippi 39205
Nuts

Sugarbush Farm, Inc.
RFD. 2
Woodstock, Vermont 05091
Candies, cheese, maple syrup, maple sugar

Sunnyland Farms
Route 1, Box 998
Albany, Georgia 31702
Candies, fruitcake, dried dates, ham, nuts

Sunray Orchards
Route 1, Box 299
Myrtle Creek, Oregon 97457
Dried prunes

Swiss Cheese Shops
Highway 69N
Monroe, Wisconsin 53566
Cheese

The Swiss Colony
1112 Seventh Avenue
Monroe, Wisconsin 53566
Cakes, candies, cheese, cookies, fruitcake, honey, smoked duck, meats, nuts, preserves, puddings, tea

Thousand Island Apiaries
Route 2
Clayton, New York 13624
Honey

The E. M. Todd Co.
Box 5167
Richmond, Virginia 23220
Bacon, ham

The Vermont Country Store
Weston, Vermont 05161
Maple syrup, maple candy, cheese, mincemeat, whole grains

Vermont General Store
Woodstock, Vermont 05091
Natural and organic foods, syrups

Vita Green Farms
P.O. Box 878
Vista, California 92083
Dried fruits, nuts, rice, natural and organic foods

Walnut Acres
Penns Creek, Pennsylvania 17862
Natural and organic foods

Weaver's
Box 525
Lebanon, Pennsylvania 17042
Bacon, ham, dried beef, bologna, meat gift packages

Wide World of Herbs
11 St. Catherine Street East
Montreal, Canada
Herbs, spices

Joe Williams
Camden, Alabama 36726
Nuts

Wonder Natural Foods
11711 Redwood Highway
Wonder, Oregon 97543
Pollen

Young Pecan Sales Corp.
P.O. Box 632
Florence, South Carolina 29501
Nuts

The Mail-Order

FOOD

Book

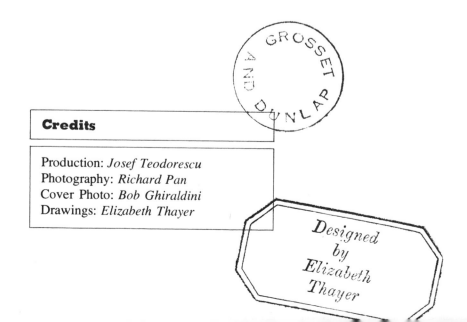

GROSSET AND DUNLAP

Credits

Production: *Josef Teodorescu*
Photography: *Richard Pan*
Cover Photo: *Bob Ghiraldini*
Drawings: *Elizabeth Thayer*

Designed
by
*Elizabeth
Thayer*